MW01101173

Colors Beneath the Veil

COLORS
BENEATH
THE VEIL

Inspiring Reflections of an
American Girl's Journey to Iran

TAMMY BLENKUSH

Colors Beneath the Veil: *Inspiring Reflections of an American Girl's Journey to Iran*
Copyright Pending 2005, Tammy Blenkush

First Edition
Printed in USA
ISBN 0-9762518-0-9

Published by Ebony Publishing Company
For inquires and comments contact:
Ebony Rose Publishing Company
P.O. Box 5040
Central Point, OR 97520
EbonyRosePubCo@aol.com

Acknowledgements: The author gratefully acknowledges and thanks the following people for their assistance and contributions to the production of this book.

Cover Design: Eric Warren, Rogue Design

Interior Design: Shannon Bodie, Lightbourne, Inc.

Proof Reading Assistance: Barbara Hedman

The following poetry selections from *The Gift*, by Daniel Ladinsky.
Copyright © 1999. Reprinted by permission of the author.

Page 19 - What is this precious love. Page 77 - The Vintage man. Page 121 - It Felt Love. Page 199 - Two Giant Fat People. Page 228 - The Thousand-Stringed Instrument (the last verse). Page 312 - Stealing Back the Flute.

The poem, I picked one rose in a hurry, from *Crazy As We Are: Selected Rubais from the Divan-i Kebir of Meviana Celaeddin Rumi*, Translated by Dr. Nevit O. Ergin, Prescott, Arizona: Holms Press, 1992, page 39, used with permissions.

Poetry credit: Persian Poets, Selected by Peter Washington. Publisher Alfred A. Knopf. Page 174. "The Lessons of the Flower" (last verse).

Disclaimers: Some of the people's names herin may have been changed. And the names of many places and monuments identified in this book were changed after the 1979 Revolution. The author's ideas and opinions herin do not necessarily reflect the ideas and opinions of those persons mentioned in this book.

CONTENTS

Look at it from orbit
Look at it that far
Look for brother and your love
God is bigger than in your heart

Look at it from orbit
Look at it with love
See how is the frame
How is life

See yourself down on earth
So small
Look at it bigger than Love
Look at it with God

—*Mehradad*
(my Iranian friend)

INTRODUCTION

SPIRIT OF INSPIRATION

TRAVELING THE COUNTRY ROADS of Southern Oregon and Northern California as a Sales Representative, I worked my way from one customer to another, through city after city, silently watching my life go by. With only the view out the window, music from the stereo and my thoughts to keep me amused, I'd often wonder how I could find time in such a hectic world to fulfill my lifetime dream. I always dreamed of touching the lives of others by revealing my personal reflections of life through my art and words.

One quiet winter morning while I wound along Highway 101 through the enchanting redwood forest, watching sunlight filter through trees and flicker off my windshield, the insight suddenly struck me. "I don't have to watch my life go by from a window, or keep my dream buried inside. I can use my time traveling to note down my thoughts, and then write a book that shares the voice of my heart with others. The spirit of this book would be to enrich lives and inspire others to follow their hearts and fulfill their dreams." Once this vision came to me, the question of how I could realize my dream was instantly erased from my mind. And that, in all its simplicity, planted the seed for this book.

The remainder of that insightful day, I struggled to push the idea of writing a book aside and shift my focus back to the reality of my daily work. No matter how hard I tried to focus, though, the vision of writing gradually returned, captivating my thoughts all over again. With so many ideas tumbling through my mind, how could I get my ideas on paper quickly or clearly enough to be understood, let alone to write a book? What was the magical formula? What specifically would I write about and where would I begin?

Throughout the next several months ideas came and went about how I could compose my book, but none of them seemed to flow, as they should, from my mind, through the pen, on to the empty pages.

Then, one warm Sunday afternoon, standing in front of my mirror and working another handful of the dark green mud through my slightly salt-and-pepper hair, I began wondering how the yucky color of henna dye could turn in to such brilliant hues of red highlighting in my hair. That's when memories began to surface of the first time I saw the ancient art used—how the hair sparkled as the sun touched, and then reflected off the Persian women's radiant colors of mahogany and auburn henna-dyed hair.

At that moment, the spark, the light, the idea of how I would write this book shone through. After months of struggling and searching to find an answer, the inspiration came to me—suddenly, spontaneously and clearly. The answer, hidden, but present all along, reflected in the mirror. The wrinkles and gray hair looked back to me, but past them I saw reflections of what I would write. This came from within, from scattered pictures of the past remaining in my mind. Reflections only I could see surfaced from deep inside my heart of the magical ten-month journey to Iran many years ago that had tested my way of life, giving me a different perspective by teaching me new ways, new beliefs and new lessons. The purpose of my experience seemed to be to share my story with others—a story about a journey that had never truly ended with its passage, but in many ways, had only just begun.

And as these memories surfaced, it occurred to me that I'd been looking outside myself for a spark of inspiration to bring my book to life. Yet no matter how hard I searched, the inspiration wouldn't come. It wasn't until I looked within that I finally realized the magical inspiration I longed to find was right before my eyes, right in front of me, within the reflection in the mirror.

Yes, the world was abundant with people, places, and things to inspire me and bring color to my life, but how I saw the world could come only from inside. Other people, places, and things had been there, but for the inspiration to come to life a spark had to ignite a flame of passion inside of me that disrupted the quiet balance of my soul. This passion is what created the light that brought my dream to life.

Now I realize my heart was lighting the way all along. Yes, my heart knew where to start. My heart knew where to go. All I needed to do was trust my heart and follow the path it was guiding me down. When my dream was meant to be, my mind was clear, and the time was right—the answer came, and like magic the light from within my soul shone through, illuminating the path that led me to the inspiration for writing this book.

But this book isn't only about my story. This book is a reflection of the amazing gift of grace God has given each of us. A gift, which over time, gently teaches us that we are not only our physical presence, we are our spirit too, that delicate seed in our soul. Our body is only the instrument used to reflect the heart of our spirit, which is filled with the colorful lessons of love. But this gift of grace can shine only when we begin to reveal this love by surrendering it to the universe around us—when we begin to see the world spiritually, when we begin to see the world not only through our eyes, but through our hearts too.

So use your body as it's intended to be used. Remember your body has a purpose too. Your body is the instrument used to reflect your spirit—a spirit that moves, that shines, that touches and brings love to others as it reflects the grace that moves your soul. Share your story of love with the world. Share it from the heart. Use your body to reveal who you really are. Share your story in bits and pieces, if necessary. Tell your story with humor, joy, and lightheartedness. Tell your story with zip, pizzazz and passion. Tell your story with despair, fear and sorrow—if that's the kind of story you have. You know how to tell your story, the way it comes from your heart—the way it feels and touches your soul. Don't worry about how simple, complicated, long or short your story may be, or in what shape or form you choose to express it. Let your spirit move your body toward what it's intended to do, which is to share your gift of grace with the world.

Through this you, too, may discover how your experiences of yesterday are a part of you today. And how the lessons from these experiences give you the wisdom and the strength to carry you through tomorrow. So respect the lessons learned each and every moment of your life. Cherish the past for what it means to you today; accept it for what it was yesterday. Feel the emotions and find the inspiration in each experience that has touched your life. Then, if need be, let it go, be at peace with the past; accept with faith that yesterday was meant to be. It helped paint the colors of your heart today.

With this, I invite you to follow me through the pages of this book on a magical journey into my heart. Where I bring to light my true experience as an idealistic American girl living in Iran, by narrating the story through my eyes and my heart as I was then, when I was only seventeen years old. Although many memories have faded over time, some are still clearly etched in my mind. I've filled the pages of this book with these memories, and then reflected on one of the most inspirational experiences of my life to show you how yesterday's journey helped paint the colors of my heart today. This story also tells you how the experience still touches and inspires me as my passage through life continues on.

I hope my writing sparks your imagination in some small way, so you can find clarity and gain perspective from the stories in your life. And see for yourself how God gently speaks to you and inspires you with the magic and wonderment that is there, right before your eyes, every single day.

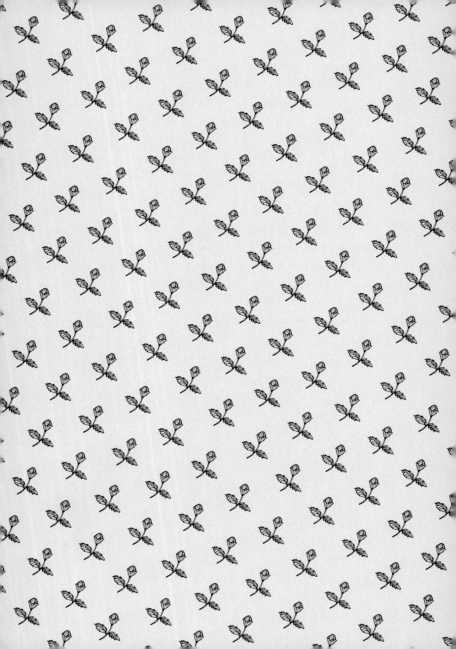

PEOPLE IN MY LIFE

THE FAMILY I LIVED WITH in Iran will always hold a cherished place in my heart. And, the amazing role each of them played in my life will live on in my mind forever. They were there to add color to my journey. They walked beside me, we broke bread together, we strolled down the same streets together to the same destinations, and we went through the same experiences together. They were there to share their lives with me, just as I was there to share my life with them. But we each have our own words, our own eyes, and our own hearts to describe what we saw, how we felt, and what was placed in our souls through our travels. Even though others were there seeing what I saw, they saw it in a different light, from a different perspective, from a different soul and through different eyes.

So I write about each family member only modestly throughout this book, not only to simplify my story but, also, because I realize we each have our own personal account of our adventure in Iran. At this point, though, I believe I should identify each person I write about and clarify his or her role in my life. This will give you a brief background of the circumstances that lead me to journey to Iran.

Ed is the stepfather of Shawn, age 23, and Vance and Damon, age 17; Vance and Damon are fraternal twins. After divorcing the boys' mother, Ed moved on and eventually began working for Bell Helicopter International as an Electronic Engineer in Isfahan, Iran. Ed lived in Iran for two years before our arrival. During that time Ed met and married Nancy, an American woman and very gifted artist from Texas. Nancy worked for a United States company as an Instructional Flight teacher for the Iranian Air Force. She had lived in Iran for four years with her three children from a previous marriage: her son Kurt, age 14 and her two daughters, Lynn, age 17, and Heather age 4. Prior to our arrival Lynn moved into an apartment with a friend, so she was absent during most of the experiences we went through as a family.

Shawn, Vance and Damon, as well as their younger brother and their mother, were all my next-door neighbors in a small town in Southern Oregon. At age 16, Vance and I became teenage sweethearts. When Ed invited his three older sons to join him in Iran, Vance was excited about going, but hesitated, not wanting to leave me behind. After Vance discussed our relationship with his father, I was invited to live with him and his family in Iran. But only after lengthy overseas telephone conversations with Ed did my mother finally approve of my move.

From that moment on, my life became a whirlwind of arrangements. My mother signed custody papers, naming Ed as my legal guardian. Passport pictures were taken. And Vance, Damon, and I received a series of shots that could only be administered by a doctor in a town sixty-five miles away from our home—a trip we made three times before our immunizations to travel overseas were complete. To this day, and forever, I'll visibly be reminded of those vaccinations from the small pox shot that bubbled up, and then healed, leaving a faint, heart shaped scar on my arm. Our trip to Iran finally became a reality when we received our passports with the official seal of the United States stamped on them, giving us the necessary authorization to travel overseas. Vance, Damon and I were off to Iran the beginning of April, 1978. Shawn followed three months later in July.

Vance, Damon, and I traveled to Iran with limited information about the people or the country to prepare us for the trip. Only short, outdated descriptions of its history existed in local libraries under the country's old name—Persia—which was changed to Iran in 1935 by Reza Shah, the first king of the Pahlavi dynasty. But Persia brought to mind, only endless desert sand, fluffy longhaired cats, humpback camels, and exotic images of paradise with make believe harem girls and turbaned men flying on colorful fringed carpets. Our friends seemed as mystified about Iran's history as we were. Their first response was, "Iran, where's that? I've never heard of that country."

But the world soon learned of Iran's existence when it arose to the forefront of world news in the fall of 1978 with sky rocketing oil prices and long lines of cars at the gas pumps. This crisis was created by striking Iranian oil workers, who believed they were doing their part for their country and for Islam in rising up against the Shah of Iran and his state policies. This event brought to light the small, oil rich country's economical impact on the United States and other countries throughout the world, all of whom partially depended on Iran's petroleum for economical survival.

The oil crisis was soon followed by the overthrow of the Shah and his government in January 1979 by the exiled Ayatollah Khomeini and his Islamic Revolution. In the fall of that same year, fifty-two Americans were taken hostage by Islamic fundamentalists at the American Embassy in the city of Tehran. The seizure at the Embassy was followed by a secret and heroic rescue attempt of the hostages by the U.S. Military under the direction of President Jimmy Carter and his administration. This rescue attempt sadly left eight American servicemen dead and the hostages no closer to home.

Only after fruitless attempts to gain freedom for the hostages did President Carter, along with the rest of the world, finally watch their release come, four-hundred and forty-four days after their capture—the day Ronald Reagan was sworn into office as the fortieth President of the United States. The timing of the hostages' release was an event not only meant to humiliate Carter, but also to make a direct political statement throughout the world of the Muslim fundamentalists hatred of the west and its ideology.

These riveting events caught the attention of the world, painting a black-and-white picture from which many frame their intolerant view of Iran. Through the mind-set of the world, Iran is connected to war, oil, terrorists, hostages, and religious fanatics. My mind-set is different, though, because I walked on Persian soil, living and breathing among the Iranian people.

I learned through this experience, how easy some of us can paint a black-and-white picture of others from a single issue in life. We may adamantly say, "This is who I believe this person is—because of this or that, and I won't change my mind." We may look at the issue from a black-and-white mind-set, leaving no room in our hearts for validating others thoughts or feelings. We forget that black-and-white, blended, creates gray, the place in the middle, the place inbetween, the place where the issues in the world around us disappear and humanity steps in.

When we focus only on the issues in life we may unconsciously create a picture that omits the colors of light—light filled with hope, faith, love, and acceptance. Sometimes we need to set aside the issues and try to understand what's truly painted in another's heart. Sometimes we need to set aside the issue to see the colors of a human soul. It's these colors I hope to bring to you through the reflections of my heart, depicted in *Colors Beneath the Veil.*

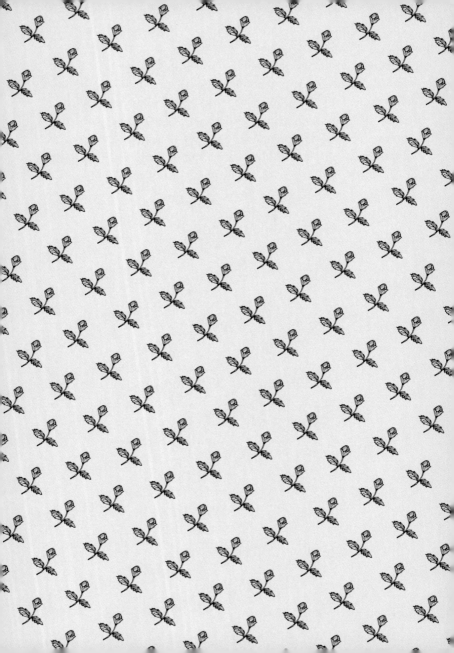

PART ONE

GOD'S GARDEN

This moral it is mine to sing:
Go learn a lesson of the flowers;
Joy's season is in life's young spring,
Then seize like them, the fleeting hours.

—Hafiz
"The Lesson of the Flower,"
from Persian Poets

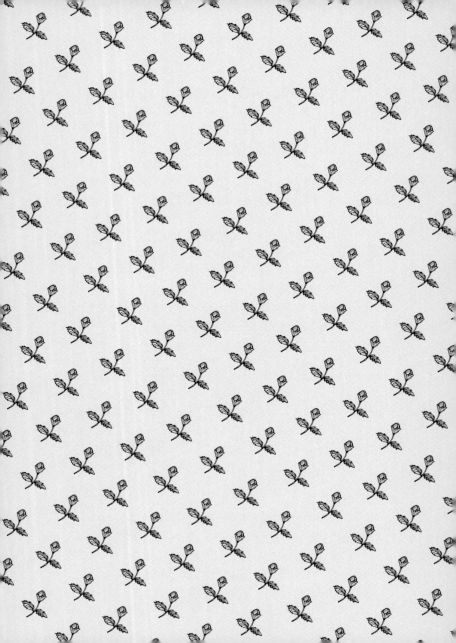

DISCOVERING GOD'S GRACE

A S A LITTLE GIRL, AT THE FIRST HINT of spring, I raced out the back door of our old white house, past the giant black walnut tree to the top of the grassy hillside. Stepping onto the rickety log that stretched over the irrigation ditch, I balanced my way to the other side. Careful not to snag my clothes, I climbed over the broken-down barbwire fence to reach the mountain's edge. There I discovered the season's first patch of purple, pink, and yellow wild flowers, freed from the earth by the warm sunshine, where they now covered the mountainside.

Pausing for a moment to absorb the array of God's beauty in his untainted garden, I wondered how the delicate seeds covered by soil could ever survive in the frozen ground of the bleak, dark winter, only to magically return and surrender their blossoms to the warmth of the sunshine and a gentle spring rain. I never quite understood God's graceful balance of nature, but with faith I accepted the reflection of His heart in the garden, all the same.

Pause for a moment. Look around. What do you see? Do you see only the bleakness of winter or maybe only the rain? Have you forgotten that after the winter comes the spring? Or after the rain comes the sunshine?

Step back and absorb the world around you. Believe life is on course, on time, working its way through the seasons of change. And, remember, it can't rain forever. If it did, the world would be only oceans. Just as the sun can't shine forever or the world would be only deserts.

Always remember your soul has seasons too. Your soul needs a little rain and a little bleakness to create the balance you need in your life for your spirit to grow. Only after the rain has fallen do we appreciate the magic and beauty the sunshine brings.

Respect each season. Appreciate its significance. Cherish the ever changing wonder each season brings. Have faith. Believe the sunshine will come, in time, naturally.

GETTING SIDETRACKED

Eager to share the precious gift of spring's delicate beginning, I picked an elegant bouquet of wild Lilies, Shooting Stars, and Lady Slippers. Then I stood back and took a second look over the flower patch to assure myself I hadn't picked too many blossoms. Once I was satisfied that you could hardly tell I'd been there, disturbing Mother Nature, I turned to make my way back down the mountain slope, only then to get sidetracked, on the top of the hill, where I stopped to rest at my favorite spot under the evergreens.

Find time on your journey to appreciate the magical splendor Mother Nature offers. It's free. The only price you pay is time, time to absorb the magic.

Sense the rich soil beneath your feet, breathe the fresh air, and hear the Earth's song. Look up, look down, and look all around you. The magic is everywhere. It has been there all along, like a treasure, waiting for you to cherish it, waiting to be found.

What's the hurry? Life doesn't always need to be met with such urgency. When we hurry, we often lose our balance, our lives become off center. We may become anxious, our minds preoccupied with tomorrow. The journey becomes unpleasant because we forget to enjoy life's magic along the way.

When we feel hurried and anxious, maybe what we need to do is stop and rest. Maybe we need to get side-tracked and wander through nature. For only a moment, we could let Mother Nature take our minds off all our labors, surrendering our body and our spirit to her magic. The tasks will still get done, the schedules will still be met, and the growth will still come. But we'll enjoy the journey along the way.

Take time to learn from Mother Nature's wisdom. She won't let you down. Instead, she'll lift your spirit. Just touch her gently. Use her sparingly. Share her magical splendor. Respect her delicate balance and she'll always be there as your friend, to give you what you need with open arms.

THE VALLEY BELOW

AFTER I PLACED THE BUNDLE OF WILDFLOWERS on a moss-covered rock sticking out from the ground, I nestled beneath the pine tree where sunlight filtered through wispy branches to warm my face. Lying there, with the scent of pine tickling my nose, I daydreamed for hours, with my cheeks placed firmly in the palms of my hands, watching life carry on without me in the valley below.

The scattered people looked so small, yet so colorful and full of life, as they moved around on the valley floor, carrying out their daily chores. As if in harmony with nature, each person seemed to have a special place and a purpose in the world—balancing the Earth and helping it whirl around.

We all have a special purpose in this world. We were each created to be who we are for a reason. We even have a calling: to live our lives to their fullest potential through the endless possibilities presented to us from the universe.

So if you're struggling to be someone other than who you are, it's unnecessary. Who you are is just fine. You are exactly who you were intended to be—in body, mind, and spirit. Over time, your spirit will grow as you learn life's lessons along the way. That growth will happen naturally. So, relax and be yourself, that person who yearns to be free from other's expectations of who you are or who you should be.

Pause for a moment. Look deep inside yourself and find those special gifts you have to offer the world. Now look outside at the universe and all it has placed before you. This is where you'll use your gifts, fill your spot, and help create harmony and balance in the world from your own special place on Earth.

My Favorite Spot

From atop the hill I saw the blue jeans and bed sheets my mother hung on the clothesline, flapping dry in the warm spring breeze. While dad, dressed in his red flannel shirt and black trousers cinched with a worn-out leather belt, chopped kindling in the woodpile.

My brother Mike's old, rusted pick-up truck sat buried in the thick of blackberry bushes. Behind the truck, our small black dog, Peanuts, desperately tried to break free from the chain that bound him to a flowering plum tree in the backyard. Peanuts seemed to run around in circles, endlessly barking at bees that swarmed the tree's blossoms. In quiet contrast, the neighbor's cows and horses grazed freely on dandelion-speckled pastures nearby.

Across the street, next to George Perry's auto repair shop, stood the local fire station with its vintage red fire truck parked inside the tarnished metal building. Mr. Perry would occasionally start the engine, pull out the fire truck, and, as it spit and sputtered, he'd turn the lights and siren on to make sure it was still in good running condition. The sound of the truck's motor revving and the blowing sirens instantly disturbed the peaceful rhythm of the quiet countryside.

At the other end of the valley, gray smoke from the sawmill burner billowed out, evaporating into the sky. Random bird chirps and dog barks were drowned out by the sound of a log truck rumbling by, and then disappearing as it crossed the green arched bridge over the Applegate River. This river was where my brothers, sisters, and I swam, skipped rocks, rolled logs, and caught crawdads with our friends in the summertime.

Find your favorite spot—the peak of a mountain, a rooftop in the city, a rock by the sea. Maybe your favorite spot is in your garden or relaxing on your front porch in an old rocking chair. Your favorite spot is wherever you want it to be. Go there often. This is where you can find peace and balance. This is where, if only for a moment, you can watch life move on, while you sit still and daydream of the endless possibilities in the world.

Be still and rest there. See how life moves and changes with each breath of the breeze. See how life flaps and flows toward freedom. Understand that you, too, are a part of this beautiful picture. Feel life's rhythm flow through you with ease, with grace, and with purpose. Then surrender to life's rhythm with all your heart, mind, body, and soul. Know without doubt, without hesitation, this is how your spirit is meant to flow.

Carry this simple thought with you every single day. And always remember that you're free to feel what you need to feel, and be all you can be, in this boundless universe of endless possibilities.

Reverend Johnson

DOWN THE ROAD BETWEEN THE SCHOOLYARD and the country store that looked like a big red barn, stood the little white church with a steeple where Rev. Johnson gave his Sunday sermons. Stomping his feet on the hardwood floor, he'd raise his powerful voice and preach with certainty of the sins that would throw us all into the darkness of hell. Then, as Mrs. Young began to play the organ, Rev. Johnson lowered his voice and softly spoke in rhythm with the music, glorifying the righteous souls who would attain everlasting life in God's beautiful garden in the hereafter. He spoke not so much about God's love, but about God's rules. I knew Rev. Johnson's intentions were well meant, but his words placed a quiet fear of God deep inside my soul, a God so different from the one I knew. Somehow, Rev. Johnson's sermons made me believe hell was much more realistic than heaven. His words left me no light to hold onto. The light I saw was the color of God's garden on the mountain.

This was my world, my life, right there in front of me, framed in evergreen-laced mountains touching the blue sky.

I believe God is right there in front of me and He has been all along. I just open my eyes and look around, and I can

see and feel God's love moving in rhythm with the universe.

I don't believe God stomps His feet or raises His powerful voice every Sunday. I believe God quietly walks beside us and gently speaks as He teaches us, day after day, about the power of love, love that doesn't force us to do the righteous thing from a set of rules or a fear of hell. God's love teaches us that in the face of everything, including the rules and the fear of hell, to instinctively do the righteous thing from our own conscience out of love.

Sometimes, though, others try to place fear in us by teaching only a dark side of God. They teach and cause fear in us, not love. If we listen and believe everything others say, we may miss the true meaning of God's light. If we listen to them, all we may understand are rules and fear. And all we may see is the darkness of hell.

If the fear of God moves in your soul, look beyond that fear to the light, and then let go of the rules that shame and repress you. Instead of looking at God through a dark side of fear, look at God through the love in your eyes. Let peace come to you, and then you will begin to understand and cherish the color of God's light on the mountain.

WILD FLOWERS

A BLUE-BELLIED LIZARD SUDDENLY DARTED from nearby, startling me back into reality. Remembering the bundle of wildflowers, I quickly gathered them up, squeezing the stems tightly in my hand, so I wouldn't lose any of them. I continued down the hill and in to the back door of my kitchen.

Holding the drooping flowers behind my back, I called with excitement, "Mama, come see what I found!"

When my mother entered the room, I called out, "Surprise!" giggling as I reached forward to hand her the wilted bouquet.

Her eyes lit up. "Oh, what beautiful flowers!" she said. "They look a little thirsty, though. Let's give them some water, and they'll be refreshed and back to life in no time."

Drying her hands on her apron, Mother took the flowers from my hand and placed them in an old Mason jar filled with water. Then she sat them on the kitchen windowsill above the sink. Sure enough, in no time at all, a sweet fragrance filled the room as the flowers gracefully unfolded their colorful blossoms, creating a beautiful display, for all to see, in our kitchen.

Just as nature thirsts for water, our spirits do, too. Our spirits need water to live, to survive, to grow, and to

blossom, just as the wildflowers do. But our spirits thirst for water for our souls. This is water that can be poured or sprinkled from one person to another through a kind word, a caring hand, or a loving thought. This water is the water of love. When our spirits are nurtured, we gently open up, sharing this love with others as our hearts blossom.

Nurture someone's spirit. Let them know they have a beautiful smile and watch them smile more often. Hug them and watch them embrace others more often. Touch someone's spirit naturally by giving him or her what they thirst for. Then, watch their spirit come to life as they display the colors of their heart in all they do and say because they thirst for love no more.

Take time to see within each soul you cross, not only the physical thirst, but the spiritual thirst, too. Remember the wildflowers. Keep the picture fresh in your mind. This will remind you of all you need to do to understand and nurture love. Then stand back and watch the blossoms of love magically unfold.

PART TWO

OUR JOURNEY BEGINS

What is this precious love and laughter
Budding in our hearts?
It is the glorious sound
Of a soul waking up!

—*Hafiz, from* The Gift

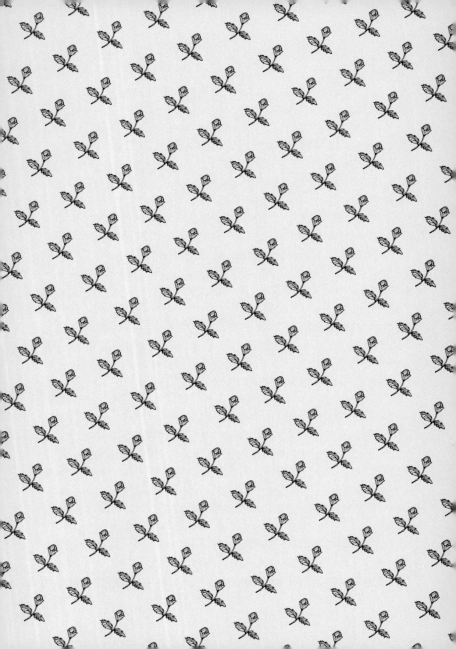

SEARCHING FOR THE ANSWER

A WARM SPRING BREEZE BLEW AGAINST my face as I made my way to the top of the hillside. As I looked out over the valley, I saw how different this year was from the years before, and realized how much the world around me had changed and moved forward since I was a little girl.

The old, rusted, pick-up truck had long since been hauled away and a dryer on the porch replaced the clothesline in the backyard. The fire truck at Mr. Perry's repair shop spit and sputtered no more. The sawmill lay quiet and still down the road. The trips to the river weren't as frequent, and Rev. Johnson's voice seemed to tremble as his feet shuffled on the floor. The only thing that remained the same was the rebirth of wildflowers in the spring.

But this spring I came to the mountain, not as a little girl searching for flowers, but as a young woman searching for the answer to why I would want to leave my peaceful life in the valley behind. My heart and mind seemed at war, searching for the answer to bring peace to my soul. In my mind I knew I was young, with my whole life ahead of me and thirsty for something new to refresh my spirit. But to move far away from home with Vance and his family, to a country I never before knew existed—that I couldn't even imagine.

Yet in my heart I knew the answer. Although my mind still had doubt and questioned the journey ahead, the quiet tugs at my heart were too hard to ignore. They gently surfaced to reassure and remind me of the tall, blond, blue-eyed boy next door I'd fallen in love with. This love deep inside my heart gave me the answer. I knew I'd miss my family and life in the valley, but if I didn't go with Vance to Iran, I knew I'd miss him even more.

Finally, I reassured myself that this was the chance of a lifetime to live in another country and that we wouldn't be gone forever—only a year or two, that's all. Maybe this was the time to let everything else go and leave the valley behind for now. Maybe this was the time to add color to my life from the light on the other side of the world.

Love is powerful. Love carries us away. Love takes us to places we never dreamed of going—not only our bodies, but our souls, too. Love changes our lives. Love frees us to make decisions from our heart. Love doesn't force decisions or changes on us. Love allows us to follow our inner voice, the quiet voice inside that knows exactly what we need. The voice that silently tugs, pulls, and then pushes us forward to wherever we need to be.

Love's choices aren't always easy, though, for sometimes they put our heart and mind at war. We may not know exactly where we're going. We may feel insecure stepping into the unknown. We may be afraid of the changes our choices might bring, because we don't know what the future holds.

But our hearts speak to us quietly and they speak simple truths. Listen to your heart's soft, gentle murmurs.

Your heart knows where to go and it knows what to do. Your heart can guide you down the path you need to travel so you can learn what you need to learn, and see what you need to see. If you listen, your heart will take you to where you ultimately need to be.

Preparing for Our Journey

THE DAY VANCE, DAMON, AND I had spent weeks preparing for finally arrived: this was the day we would begin our trip half way around the world. My suitcases were carefully packed according to a list I'd made of items I thought I might need, even though I was uncertain what to pack and what to leave behind. Because I wasn't sure what kind of a life we'd be living in Iran. But, after checking my list one last time, I felt satisfied I was prepared for the trip ahead.

From our living room window I peered through a gap in the curtain, eagerly watching for Vance and Damon to appear on the well-beaten path that led from my family's home to theirs. It seemed like forever before they finally emerged from behind the blackberry bushes that draped over the barbed wire fence separating our yards. Both Vance and Damon were weighted down with suitcases and a guitar as they made their way around the narrow trail at the end of the fence that lead past our woodpile into the front yard.

I met them at the front door, and then we loaded all our luggage into my brother Ivan's Chevy Malibu. With tears of mixed joy and sadness swelling in my eyes, I hugged and kissed my family good-bye.

Ivan drove us down the familiar country road toward Medford, where we would catch our first scheduled flight en route to Iran. I watched out the window as flourishing green scenery flashed by me, and as I struggled to capture a picture of the beautiful countryside in my mind, I began to absorb the reality of how hard it was to pack my belongings and leave my life in the valley behind.

The first thing I used to do when preparing for a trip was to make a list of items I wanted to bring or I didn't want to forget, and then I'd pack my bags according to that list. Then I'd say to myself, "Maybe I should throw in an extra pair of socks or blue jeans, just in case." "There," I'd say, "now I'm ready for my journey. I'm all prepared."

Sometimes, though, no matter what we pack or how well we prepare for a trip, it isn't enough. This is because we don't always know what we're preparing for.

Now I always try to carry with me a little graciousness and a thirst for the unknown, while leaving plenty of room for bursts of fun, laughter, and the magical lessons of life. Knowing the experience will eventually show me what I forgot, what I wasn't prepared for, but this only comes as my journey unfolds.

En route to Iran

B OARDING THE AIRPLANE AT Jackson County Airport in
Medford, Oregon, Vance, Damon, and I looked back to see
Ivan and the other family members who had come to see us off.
We smiled and waved good-bye one last time, uncertain about
when we'd be back home to see them again. As we took our seats
on the plane, mixed feelings once again came over me. Even
though I was excited about the trip ahead, I didn't want to leave
my family behind. I wanted them to see what I saw. I wanted
them to experience the journey with me. But as the plane taxied
down the runway that foggy spring morning, I realized for the
first time I'd be experiencing this part of my life without my family. There was no turning back now. In only a few days, I'd begin
a new life with Vance, Damon, and their father in Iran.

That evening our flight touched down in Dallas, Texas, where
we stayed the night at a fancy hotel near the airport. The next
morning we were led to the hotel's conference room, and then
introduced to our chaperons and the others who would accompany us throughout our travels. After being briefed on what to expect
on our trip we were each given bright yellow Bell Helicopter caps,
which we were to wear at all times, so our chaperons could easily
spot us on the plane or at a distance in the airport terminals.

From Texas we flew to New York's John F. Kennedy Airport
where we boarded a Boeing 747 airplane, the official fleet of Iran

Air. Then off we flew to Paris, where we wandered through the perfume-filled air in the airport gift boutiques and caught a glimpse of the world famous Eiffel Tower through huge windows that decorated the airport lobby. After our long layover in Paris, we once again boarded Iran Air. We then flew to Istanbul, Turkey, for a short stop, and then, at last, on to Iran.

We occasionally want others to join us on our journey through life or vice versa. We want them to see what we see. We want them to walk with us, down our path. But, sometimes, we need to let go and go places where others can't follow. Not only physically, but in our minds and hearts, too.

Sometimes others might hitch a ride with us on our journey but, in doing so, they may relinquish their life and what they need to learn. They get sidetracked down our path and, for a while, fail to follow their own hearts. They become a quiet spectator in our life. But after a while they may get bored, frustrated, or resentful when they realize their lives are passing by.

So sometimes we need to leave behind people and places we love in order to begin a new life. We need to say good-bye. But this doesn't mean the good-bye is forever. Sometimes it's only for a while, so we can learn our lessons, fulfill our dreams, and discover our own purpose in life. Then, maybe some day our paths with those we've left behind will join again, down the road, just around the corner, or on the other side of life.

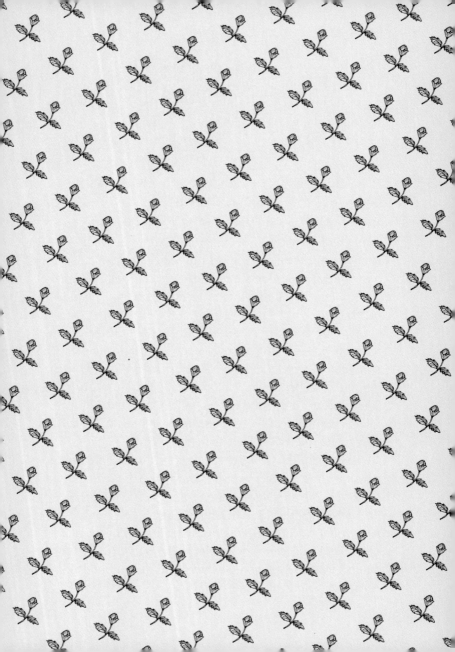

PART THREE

IRAN

God
And I have become
Like two giant fat people
Living in a
Tiny boat.
We
Keep
Bumping into each other and
L
a
u
g
h
i
n
g
.

—Hafiz, from The Gift

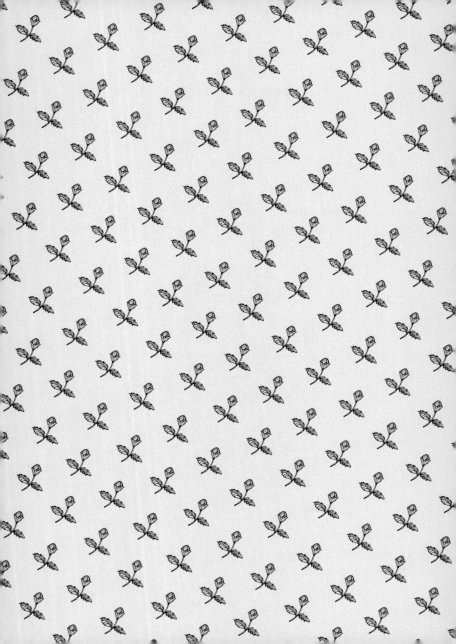

A Change of Colors

I T SEEMS A LIFETIME HAS PASSED since that clear April evening when I peered out the airplane's tiny porthole window to view city lights illuminating the sky into a golden-bronze hue over the ancient buildings below. A carefree American girl of seventeen years old, I only then began to grasp the concept of being a world away from my country and the small town in Southern Oregon where I'd grown up and called home.

As the plane descended over the city, an air of seriousness began to replace the relaxed atmosphere around us. Several Iranian women on board quickly covered their heads with scarves. A fashionably dressed young woman seated across the aisle from Vance and me wiped red lipstick from her lips, and then pulled on a *manteaus*—a cumbersome long, black overcoat often used as a body cover by Muslim women. The coat concealed her curvy figure, highlighted in a pair of designer jeans and a form-fitting blouse. Finally, she drew a silk scarf from her bag and placed it over her dark hair. She loosely tied it below her chin, leaving only her classy, high-heeled sandals to suggest any hint of western fashion. The young woman's ordinary image transformed right before our eyes. But, even at that peculiar moment, I was still unaware of how my first step off the plane onto Persian soil that warm spring evening would be the beginning of a journey that would change my perspective of life forever.

Sometimes we're blind to what might lie ahead. We don't realize when we make the choices we do how great an impact those choices could have on our lives. We often make choices believing we know what the outcome will be and yet, the outcome doesn't turn out as we expected. Yet, the outcome of other choices we make surprises us. They throw us off balance and spin us around, inspiring us when we least expect it. They lead us down a path we never imagined could open or even be there, filling our lives with the awe of something new and unimaginable. And filling our hearts with a flicker of color we never knew existed.

So don't be afraid to make choices from your heart because you never know what magic those choices might bring. Those choices could transform the colors in your heart forever.

First View

As we made our way down the boarding steps into the clear night, a dignified-looking Iranian man in front of us—dressed in a black business suit and matching shiny shoes—suddenly stopped, and then knelt and kissed the Earth we were about to step on. I assumed this gentleman was happy to be home in Iran, even though his way of expressing this was very strange to me.

A dusty odor engulfed the air as we tagged behind our chaperons across the runway. With luggage and guitars draped over our shoulders, we seemed to tread onward for miles before we finally stepped into Tehran's Mehradad International Airport.

Inside the terminal, an emotional crowd of hundreds of Iranians instantly caught us off guard. Only thick, black ropes guided us through them as they chaotically yelled and waved their hands in the air, as if they were pointing and reaching toward us. We didn't understand what was happening or why our presence seemed to create such a commotion. Our concern made us ask each other what was happening. Should we smile and wave back? Should we lower our heads in embarrassment? Or, should we ignore them? Were the Iranians welcoming us or did they dislike our being there? "Hey! Maybe they think we're rock and roll stars," Damon whispered to Vance and me—half-serious and half-joking—but at that moment, we all realized anything was possible.

Only when the dark-haired, olive-skinned people took notice

of Vance and Damon did a deafening silence fall over the crowd. As hundreds of large brown eyes stared in fascination at Vance and Damon's fair complexions, blue eyes, and vanilla-cream-colored hair beneath their yellow caps. The people's eyes remained fixated as, one by one, we slowly moved forward through the crowd.

I felt an uneasiness sweep over my body as I began to absorb the surroundings of the cold, dark, and dreary terminal. Its backdrop left little assurance to the season outside with its dark hues of blacks, browns, and dusty reds. Pictures of the Shah of Iran—crowned and seated in his peacock throne—proudly hung on walls everywhere, as if we should be honored by the very presence of his portrait. No colorful neon lights flashed to give us direction, only signs scribbled in black and red words that we couldn't read, and people rushing about us, babbling in a language we didn't understand.

My first glimpse of Iran was bleak. And the dispiriting welcome wasn't at all what I'd expected. I turned around for a moment, wondering if the plane was still there. I thought, maybe I can catch the next flight back home. But realistically I knew returning home wouldn't be that easy. It wouldn't be like girl scout camp when I called my mother to come pick me up because I was scared and didn't like it, only for her to encourage me to try camp one more day, reassuring me that if I was still unhappy then, she'd be there the very next day to pick me up and take me home.

So I decided that today was too early for me to judge how our new life in Iran would be. I brushed the thought of going home from my mind as the three of us walked on.

Now and then we may find ourselves in unfamiliar places. We might move to a new city, far away from family and friends, or start a new job with different responsibilities and different people in unfamiliar surroundings. Before we give the new circumstances a chance, we may say, "I don't like it here—nothing seems familiar, I'm uncomfortable, and I feel out of place."

But maybe we can say, "I'll give it one more chance— I'll give it one more day" instead? This doesn't mean to ignore your inner voice or your intuition. You will know when a situation isn't right for you. You will know when it's time to leave. But give the situation enough time to know which way you really need to go.

The Iranian Way

W E BEGAN MAKING OUR WAY ACROSS the lobby's dimly lit cement floor toward the restrooms when I noticed a group of Iranian women clustered together, squatting in a circle on the floor. Each woman wore what looked like a long black sheet (a chador), loosely wrapped around her from head to toe. Only deep, dark ebony eyes pierced from beneath the veils, silently following and absorbing our every move as we passed by.

I smelled a strong odor of urine in the air as we approached the restrooms. The stalls were filthy. Toilets had overflowed onto the floor, several lay flipped over on their sides, and the stalls had no doors to conceal the mucky mess. All the other stalls were occupied, except for one at the end of the row. I lightly pushed open the wobbly, hinged door and peeked inside. To my surprise, what I saw wasn't a toilet at all, at least not any toilet I'd ever seen. I stood there, baffled, unsure what to think of that hole in the floor with a white porcelain frame. Yet, the more I examined its shape, the more it began to look like a toilet, only set flush to the ground. Realizing I didn't have much of a choice but to use this strange-looking thing, I stepped inside the stall and closed the door behind me. Vance and Damon stood guard outside and held the door shut. Careful not to touch my jeans on the yucky ground, I squatted over the hole and quickly put it to use. When I finished, I turned to reach for the toilet paper, but there was none and I saw no real sign any had ever been there. No spindles on the wall, no empty paper rolls, not even a scrap of tissue lay on the floor.

Dripping dry, I began to justify my experiences in Iran so far. I reassured myself that the crowd of people yelling and waving as we entered the terminal were only happy to see Americans visiting their country, and all the commotion they created was simply their way of welcoming us to Iran. And the toilet thing—well, using it wasn't really any different than squatting in the woods back home. I finally reassured myself that everything would be okay. I needed only to adjust to a few little differences, that's all.

Some of us may walk into the privacy of a person's world, and then assume that person's manner, way of life, or surroundings isn't as it should be. We may say, "This isn't the way you should live your life. This isn't the way life should be. That isn't the proper way to behave or believe." But maybe what we're really saying is, "You should live and act as I do. I know the right way to live and what's best for your life." Somehow, we assume our way of life is the only righteous way.

We may forget that each person, each country, and each culture has their own unique ways. Their own unique ways to act and believe. Their own unique manners and charm. And their own unique place and purpose in this world.

What we believe is important in our lives may not be what others believe is important in their lives.

Sometimes we simply need to take a deep breath, calm our thoughts and nerves, accept others' ways, and respect their differences as we learn to adjust to a few little differences in the world around us.

THE CHADOR

E XITING THE RESTROOM HUMBLED and still a bit confused, my attention was suddenly drawn to an outburst across the way. The sound was so familiar, yet so contrary to the dark and heartless place surrounding me. And the sound radiated forth from the most unsuspecting place—from within the crowd of mysterious women shrouded in black we'd passed. I watched from a distance as the women's hands fidgeted beneath their chadors to keep them in place, while their ebony eyes lit up in joy as the sound of laughter filled the air with brilliant hues of color, sparkling all around them. My heart began to soften. A gentle peace came over me, replacing my uneasiness with comfort as I listened to the familiar sound of laughter and felt the common bond of joy. At that moment, a colorful life began unfolding all around me that I couldn't see—I could only sense it, living in the hearts beneath the veils.

Comfort comes from within us. Comfort is where our minds and bodies go when we feel at ease, at peace, and at home. Laughter fills the air with comfort. We hear it, we smile, and, for a moment, we forget about the darkness in the world around us.

Like magic, laughter fills our hearts with the colors of joy. So, when life seems dark and dreary, look for the colors. Look for the colors that can't be seen—the colors of the heart.

We all carry the power to reflect this universal bond of joy through the sound of laughter. Use this power often. It's easy. Don't hold back. You never know who could be listening. The sound of laughter may be just what that person needs to bring him comfort or to help her feel at home and at peace.

ISFAHAN

THE TURBULENT, ONE-HOUR FLIGHT south from Tehran to the town of Isfahan, buried deep inside Iran's borders, was the final destination of our long journey. No welcoming display of city lights were seen out in the middle of the flat barren wasteland. The pilot began circling the sky before slowly descending toward a few flickering lights that lit the airport runway. As the plane touched the ground an overwhelming feeling of excitement rippled through me, followed by a sense of relief that we'd finally reached our destination.

A faint scent of sandalwood freshened the stale air around us as we entered Isfahan's airport terminal. The lobby was quiet with only a few Iranian men strolling about the grounds. They seemed unruffled by our presence. The laid-back atmosphere was strikingly different from the emotional welcome we received in Tehran.

Ed and Nancy were easy to spot across the small, dimly lit waiting area. Ed stood tall among the native Iranian men. His Philippine heritage sparkled in his eyes as he clenched a cigar in one corner of his mouth and grinned on the other side. Nancy stood next to Ed. Her fair complexion, light brown hair, and cheerful smile were a refreshing welcome from what we'd seen earlier. Knowing the culture shock we'd just experienced, I'm sure Ed and Nancy could see the relief on our faces when we saw them, waiting to greet us with open arms.

After we gathered our bags, Vance, Damon, and I followed Ed and Nancy to their cute little green, German made, Geon Jeep, which looked like a miniature military Hum-V, minus the camouflage paint. Piling the vehicle high with luggage, we squeezed into the leftover space in the back seat. Then, under a misty midnight sky, we began the 45-minute drive from the airport to our new home in the city.

As we rapidly traveled through the darkness down a lone, bumpy highway toward Isfahan, Ed began to explain to us that the street (*koche*) we would live on was once an ancient camel road used by Persian people as the main road to the market place (the Grand Bazaar) in Isfahan. The *koche* was still considered a religious and historical pathway for the Iranians because it was part of the old Silk Road, an overland route of about 4,000 miles, on which silk and other goods were carried by camel from Asia to Europe during the medieval era. Ed said we probably wouldn't see many camels in Iran because the Shah, who believed these animals made his country look uncivilized in the eyes of the west, had discouraged their use.

Ed went on to explain that he and Nancy had decided to experience life in Iran by living in the city center, instead of on the American compound located on the outskirts of town. He said they wanted to learn more about the Iranian culture and felt the only way they could do so was to live among the people. They were one of only a few foreign families who had the courage to venture out and live in the heart of Isfahan, a historical and deeply religious Shiite Muslim city in Iran.

Isfahan was well known for gifted craftsman who created block print tapestries, detailed miniature paintings, and beautiful Persian carpets. It featured the world-famous Shah's Square, the

Royal Mosque, and the Hall of Forty Pillars, which really wasn't a hall at all, nor did it have forty pillars. The monument was built in an open plaza with only twenty pillars, but its reflection in the pool of water behind it gave the illusion of having forty pillars. Ed said that because of the significance of the Forty Pillars in Iran's history, the word "forty" was a phrase often used by Iranians to mean "many." So, if you're talking to an Iranian, don't assume that when the word "forty" is spoken, it's meant to be taken literally.

The seventh-century Royal Mosque, located in Shah's Square, several blocks from where we would live, was recognized as one of the most stunning buildings in the world. The mosque reflected sounds so precisely that stomping your foot only once on the ground beneath the mosque's gigantic dome created a wave of seven equal echoes.

Isfahan was once the capital of Iran when Abbas I, the Great Shah of Persia, ruled the country in the late 1500s. Shah's Square, the city's historical central plaza, was named after the Great Shah. Along with rebuilding Persia's Empire, the king had extraordinary Islamic monuments and palaces built in and around Shah's Square, whose majestic architectural designs outshone many in the Islamic world. Consequently, most Iranians considered Isfahan the heart of the country because it still reflected much of Iran's ancient history, architecture, and spirit. This was in contrast to the country's capital, Tehran, where western influence adorned countless city boulevards.

As we crossed the Zayandeh-rud River, under the primitive arches of the sixth-century Allahverdi Bridge, a light rain began to fall. Only reflections from the headlights shining on the dampened road lit our way as we entered the city and wound our way through the eerie, dark, deserted streets. The merchants' shops were closed and locked down for the night with solid metal bars and gates. Not a soul could be seen, and the only movement was from rodents and a few mustard-colored, wild dogs (*joob* dogs) scavenging for food and water on the sparsely lit streets.

We looped and weaved our way through town, finally taking a right onto Moshir-an-sari, a dark, narrow alleyway off Hafez Street, one of the main streets in the city. Lining each side of the *koche* were tall, primitive, mud clay walls with flat roofs and doors every hundred feet or so. Each door represented an Iranian family's home. In the middle of the *koche,* we came to an abrupt stop in front of a green door. This was the entrance to Ed and Nancy's home where we would live. No front yard welcomed us. We simply stepped from the *koche* into the front door of the mud house.

I was beginning to admire Ed and Nancy for having the curiosity and courage to venture into the unknown. And for living among the Iranians, where they could feel and touch the soul of the people by simply existing in their midst.

To be part of another culture is nothing we can truly understand unless we live and breathe the same air, walk beside them on their streets, and carry on our daily lives among them. Only then do we begin to understand what the spirits of the people hold.

Libraries are abundant with books to read and movie theaters are full of scenes from places we've never been. But to be present, absorbing the energy, emotions and beliefs, is different, because it's real. It's the way life is—unedited and unrehearsed.

But our first glimpse into the unknown can be eerie. We may see only the dark side of the picture and what that darkness brings. You don't need to go to another country to see what I mean. Sometimes, others are living a lifestyle so different from our own just down the road or around the corner. So we stay away, we avoid the scene. We stay in our own world where we feel safe, blocking out another way of life as if it didn't exist.

Maybe what we're frightened of is the very thing we need to see. Maybe we need to have the courage and the curiosity to venture into the unknown. Maybe then we will see the darkness turn to light as we begin to understand others and their way of life, through the picture deep within our heart's eye.

The Light over the City

ENTERING THE HOUSE, MY ONLY thought was sleep. The three-day flight to Iran had been exciting but, also, long and exhausting. I was relieved the trip had ended and simply wanted to close my eyes and fall asleep on a soft pillow, then wakeup refreshed and see everything through the light of a new day.

Vance and I followed Ed and Nancy out a back door that led across a small cement patio, which was lit up by lights reflecting off water that sprinkled from a fountain in the center of a court-yard garden. Then we walked up a short flight of stairs leading to our bedroom. The all-white bedroom had a large, walk-in closet behind a wall covered in mirrors. A few feet across the floor from the foot of the bed were large French windows, from which we could see down into the courtyard. But it was the spectacular view Vance and I saw when we peered out over the flat rooftops throughout the whole city that caught our eyes and took our breath away. A few blocks away, under the glow of the moonlight, a soft halo lay above a glittering display of lights that reflected off shiny tiles atop an Islamic mosque's gigantic dome. The magical display was the most enchanting sight I'd ever seen—yet mystifying, as if a captivating force was drawing us near to touch and grab hold of its light.

What enchants you? What captivates you? What draws out your spirit? Perhaps you're drawn to a certain light for a specific reason. Maybe you need to discover more of what its spirit holds. Maybe you need to touch and grab hold of the light to understand the spirit beneath the scene. Or, maybe the light holds the next lesson you need to learn or the next thing you need to see. Or, perhaps the light is the very next journey you need to take.

We often believe our journey is over when we arrive at our final destination, when we can finally rest our body, mind, and spirit. And yes, that part of the journey is over, but a new one has only just begun. Another light shines as life's magical journey continues on.

An Echo over the City

T HE PICTURE OF THE MOSQUE WAS still clear in my mind when I laid my head down on the soft pillow, closed my eyes, and fell into a deep sleep. I barely began to dream when, instantly startled awake, I sprung into an upright position, listening to a loud, mystical voice echoing through the city. Frightened, and a little disoriented, I quickly hopped out of bed. The morning sunrise lit my way as I fumbled to get dressed on my way down the stairs. My bare feet touched the dewy ground as I crossed the courtyard to reach the French doors on the back of the house. I hesitated for a moment before entering the door. The mysterious sound had faded away. As I looked around, I realized there was probably a good explanation for the noise because no one else seemed bothered by the sound. Curious about what I'd heard, I entered the house anyway.

Ed was getting ready for the workday ahead, oblivious to the noise outside.

"Did you hear that sound?" I asked anxiously.

"What sound?" Ed replied.

"You couldn't have missed it. It was a loud, eerie voice echoing over the entire city."

Ed smiled, as if he were amused by my sincere innocence.

"Oh, that sound," he said. "That's the *Muezzin.* Each morning, he calls out to the people through a loud speaker in the

56

Minaret tower, high above the mosque, to remind the Muslim faithful that it's time for prayer."

Ed went on to explain that the majority of Iranians were Shiite Muslims, although Shiites were a minority throughout the rest of the Islamic world. Shiites prayed three times a day while most other Muslim sects, such as the Sunni, prayed five times a day. When the people heard the *Muezzin* call, they stopped whatever they were doing, wherever they were. They removed their shoes and kneeled on their prayer rugs to face Mecca, the city they believed to be God's house. While praying to Allah (God), the Shiites touched their hands on the ground and their foreheads on a piece of clay that came from the holy city of Karbala. The use of clay during prayer arose from the historical Sunni-Shiite rivalries in Karbala and was a custom distinctive only of Shiite Muslims.

The ritual of facing Mecca began with the founder of Islam— the Prophet Muhammad—who came some 600 years after Jesus to spread justice, equality, and peace throughout the world. The word "Islam" originated from the Arabic word "surrender." It was said that one day, Muhammad directed all Muslims to turn and face Mecca instead of Jerusalem while they prayed, after unsuccessful attempts to bring peace and harmony among Jews, Christians, and Muslims. The change of direction in prayer was a statement of Islam's independence from Judaism and Christianity. However, Muhammad never asked that Jews or Christians convert to Islam because he believed they, too, had received genuine revelations of their own from God. Muhammad respected their faith and encouraged other Muslims to do so as well. Every Muslim was expected to take a pilgrimage to Mecca at least once in his or her lifetime, unless life's circumstances prevented it. This journey was called the *hajj,* which was one of the five Pillars of Islam. The other four Pillars were offering prayer five times a day, fasting during the Ramadan holy period, giving alms to the needy, and, above all, the belief that there was no God but Allah, and Muhammad was Allah's last and final prophet. Anyone who remained faithful to those basic spiritual guidelines was considered a true Muslim, regardless of his or her beliefs.

After Ed explained some of the history of the Muslim faith to me, I felt a little silly that I'd become so worked up over the sound.

"Why didn't you tell us last night, so we'd understand what was happening when we heard the call? It was kind of spooky," I said, downplaying my fear. The sound had terrified me.

With a slight grin, Ed answered, "Because I wanted you to experience it all for yourself. That's what you're here for isn't it, for the experience?"

Now and again, others try to prepare us for the events ahead. Their intentions may be well meant, but preparing us can sometimes take the magic from an experience away. They may shout, "Don't go down that path or this will happen! Don't do that, it's too dangerous, too risky, or too chancy. Stop! Wait! Don't do that, you're unprepared." They say, "I'll guide you. I'll tell you what's going to happen next, long before you need know, long before you're going to experience it. Just listen to me, I'll keep you safe. I'll prepare you for what's ahead."

Others may take the magic, the delight, and the surprise from the moment by setting the stage and preparing us for what's ahead. They may spoil our experience before it's our own, leaving us nothing new to experience for ourselves. Others may do this without even knowing.

Sometimes, it's time to tap them on the shoulder and say, "I want to experience this life for myself. I want to see the magic, and feel the delight and surprise. Yes, I even want to feel the grief, heartache, and sorrow for myself. That's what I'm here for, isn't it—the experience—the lesson—the wonderment—the magical adventure of my life?"

OUR NEW HOME

MORNING BROKE. WIDE-AWAKE and curious about my surroundings, I began to absorb the unfamiliar world around me. Our traditional, primitive, villa-style house was built of thick-caked mud and brick walls formed in an *L* shape around a small courtyard, with a star-shaped fountain in the center. A sweet fragrance filled the air from colorful spring flowers, just beginning to bloom in garden beds that bordered tall, private walls, which separated our home from the neighbors.

The living room was decorated in exotic Middle Eastern and Oriental pictures, with an array of copper, brass, and pottery pieces scattered around. Beautiful silk and wool Persian carpets covered cement floors throughout the house, with a few antique foot-worn rugs hanging on the walls for only our eyes to see their classic designs and color softened by time. The couch or *poshti,* the traditional Iranian couch, was made of woven wool Afghani saddlebags, designed and dyed in natural earth tones—hues of orange, yellow, brown, and red. The saddlebags were stuffed to form a pillowed couch lying on the floor. Outdated *National Geographic, Time,* and *Life* magazines cluttered the floor on the other side of the couch.

Stepping out the French doors into the crisp morning air, I walked across the courtyard and back up the stairs leading to our bedroom. A small balcony sat at the top of the stairs. The bedroom of Nancy's teenage son, Kurt, was to the right. His room looked like mine and Vance's, only a door on the other side of the room led directly on to the flat rooftop outside.

Stepping across the balcony, I entered our bedroom again. As I looked out the large window, I saw in daylight what I'd seen only dimly in the dark the night before. Flat mud rooftops throughout the city were even with the floor of our room. The only other highest point visible was the Islamic mosque, but instead of the alluring halo of lights we saw in the night, the morning sunrise reflected bright blue mosaic tiles covering the Royal Mosque and its gigantic dome. The shiny tiles were painted a vivid color of turquoise, detailed in hues of yellow, blue, orange, white, black, and gold. The sunlight against the ancient mosque created a much more colorful, yet more realistic, picture than the night before.

I heard footsteps behind me. I turned around to see a little girl with sleepy blue eyes and a freckled face standing at the door.

She looked up at me and asked, "Hey, lady, what's your name?"

"My name's Tammy. What's your name?"

"Heather," she said, twirling her fire-red hair around her tiny finger.

"So, you're Heather, Nancy's little girl?"

Bashfully she nodded her head "yes."

"Do you want to see my secret hiding place?" Heather asked.

"Sure, you lead the way," I answered.

Grabbing my hand, Heather lead me back down the stairs to the entrance of Damon's bedroom, which was built underground at the foot of the stairs below our room. I followed Heather down into the darkened room, which looked more like a dungeon than a bedroom. The room had only one slender horizontal window below the ceiling for natural light to shine through. The window was at ground level on the outside and the only view from inside was the sky.

Midway back up the stairs to the right, Heather showed me her secret hiding place in a little nook next to Damon's closet. The hiding place was tucked away behind a door, invisible to the unknowing eye. Beneath the door was a small space, built in the floor under the ground. Iranian families who had once lived there used the concealed space as a hideaway during times of war or danger. Not that we would ever use it but, for some reason, I felt comforted to know the secret hiding place was there.

To one side of the living room was Ed and Nancy's bedroom. Off the other side was a long hallway with a bathroom at one end, which had a shower and a modern toilet inside. Midway up the hallway to the left was the kitchen with a few dishes in the sink. And, at the end of the hallway to the right, was a second bathroom with one of those strange Farsi toilets I'd used at the airport, only toilet paper was actually hanging from a spindle on the wall. Ed had explained that pubic restrooms were unisex and they didn't have locks on the doors, so the custom was to tap on the door before entering a stall. If you heard taps back from the other side that meant the stall was in use. Restrooms didn't provide toilet paper either, which was a luxury many poor Iranians couldn't afford. So for cleanliness, many Iranians still used their right hands to eat with and their left hands to wipe with, as they had for thousands of years.

To the right of the bathroom was the entrance to a small garage. A dirt bike, and one of Ed and Nancy's two cars, an Iranian made Paykan—was parked inside. To the left of the bathroom, at the end of the hall, was the front door where we first entered the house the night before. As I stood in front of the door, I could hear a confusing mix of bustling sounds coming from the other side.

I was beginning to feel comfortable in Ed and Nancy's house. Their home was inviting and full of charm. A place where I could sense the new and the old energy within the warmth of the mud walls surrounding me.

Fill your home with colors that warm your heart and with things that kindle your spirit. Make your home a place where friends and family can gather and sense your spiritual energy all around them, where they can relax and feel at home in their surroundings. Don't worry about magazines scattered on the floor or a few dishes in the sink. And you don't always have to be so tidy. This is where you live. It's your home. And, sometimes, a little untidiness is part of the comfort and charm.

Choose your home carefully. Find a place that comforts you—inside and out. You might like the hustle and bustle of the city or the peacefulness of the country. Or, you might choose a mansion, a cottage, or a place by the sea. Let the outside of your home reflect your heart inside, because what surrounds you on the outside fills your spirit too.

The World Outside

URIOUS ABOUT THE SOUND, I cracked open the front door and peeked outside. To my surprise, overnight the streets had come alive. Horns were blaring and people were hollering "Shalom! Shalom!" and babbling in the Persian language— Farsi—which I didn't understand. Crowds of men, women, and children scurried every which way, up and down the *koche* in front of our house.

Men and boys—rich and poor—were clothed in drab suit jackets made of a hodgepodge of fabrics and patterns. Some dressed in baggy wool or cotton drawstring pants and others in polyester trousers. Most men wore brown or black rubber sandals. A few dressed in robes and wore small caps or turbans on their heads. One man I noticed actually seemed out of place wearing a matching gray suit and black rubber sandals. I assumed he must have been an important man in the neighborhood. Although suit jackets worn by Iranian men were part of a state dress code imposed by the Shah to help modernize the country (or at least to create the appearance of modernization to the outside world), there were obviously countless variations to this rule.

Women were coming and going to market. Some carried unwrapped, fresh pieces of round, flat bread pressed beneath their arms, while crates of tiny, old-fashioned milk bottles rattled together in their hands. Many women were draped with black chadors, loosely wrapped around them, dusting the ground. Others wore solid pale-colored chadors or ones with small calico prints. A few women were dressed in fashionable clothes, with only a wool or silk scarf draped over their head and tied beneath their chin, and some wore no veil at all.

Persian women didn't always have a choice whether to wear Islamic dress. In the mid 1930s, Reza Pahlavi, the Shah of Iran, declared traditional Islamic dress unlawful and wearing it became punishable by jail. The Shah dispatched his military to towns and villages throughout Iran, where they were instructed to enforce the law by yanking chadors off women's backs and distributing western style suit jackets to men. Men weren't allowed to grow beards and most turbans were banned. But when Muhammad Reza Pahlavi became the Shah in 1941, after his father was forced out of power, he once again allowed Islamic dress. This gave a woman the right to cover herself in public if she chose to do so. Government workplaces were one of the only exceptions to the rule.

The Islamic holy book (Qur'an) nor the Prophet Muhammad required *hejab,* the traditional Islamic covering. Although, in the eyes and minds of most Iranian people, the traditional chador had come to symbolize innocence, honor, humility, power, and religious devotion. For some Iranian women, the absence of the chador in public left them feeling naked in body and spirit, and impure as women. Yet, for many others, especially the young, the affluent, and the educated, the absence of the chador symbolized their independence and freedom of choice, not only as women, but also as human beings.

I noticed even some of the little girls were caught up in the world of covering themselves. Although, as they darted from one side of their mother to the other, skipping and hopping along, their only challenge was keeping their chadors on. Their tiny hands tugged and pulled at the veils, trying hard, at least for a while, to keep the coverings in place. Then their minds wandered, forgetting the struggle, and the chadors once again tumbled from their faces. I couldn't help but smile as I watched the little girls so innocently surrender the cumbersome veils to the curiosity of their spirits, caught in the magical world all around them.

It was only when I caught sight of three mysterious women shrouded in pure black that an uneasy feeling came over me and spoiled the uplifting scene. The only way to tell the women's back from her front was a mesh screen that covered her entire face. She could see out of the mesh barrier, but no one could see in. For a moment, the sight of these women, stirring beneath the black cloaks, looked as if shadows of death were out there, lurking among the spirited crowd. (These women were members of a Muslim sect called the *Hezbollah*, whose conservative views even most Iranians considered extreme).

I began to notice some of the Iranian people passing by our front door, stopping and gawking and smiling at me, as I looked outside, gawking at them. I knew all I had to do was take one step out the door and I'd be right there, in the midst of all the hub-bub. But feeling a little awkward, I retreated inside the house and closed the door behind me. I wasn't quite ready to face that strange new world out there alone.

Watch children as they flow toward freedom. See how they enjoy each magical waking moment. Wouldn't it be wonderful if we could all be like children—pure and

innocent of heart, giving and receiving love freely without resistance? Maybe we should all try to envisage God from the eyes of a child, by capturing His wonder through our natural curiosity about the world outside. Maybe we should all try to sense God with an open mind and heart, ready to absorb all He has to offer our spirits.

If we watch closely, we will see, no matter how hard we try to prevent natural growth, the spirit leads us to what's free. No matter how others try to repress us, our spirits find a way to escape the reins of the physical world—thus freeing us to absorb the world of spiritual light surrounding us.

Yes, others may be there to offer us wisdom and help us along our spiritual path but, in the end, the lessons to be learned are our own. Others can't give us the virtues in life. These come only when we see the world through the eyes of a child. So take time to see and feel the magic of each moment. Take time to absorb the natural wonderment in the world around you. Because only then can you truly be free to see life's magic.

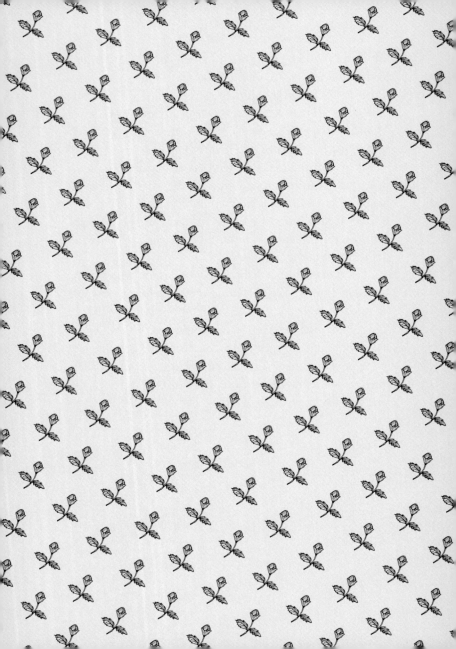

PART FOUR

MR. MOSEPORE

"The heart is
The thousand-stringed instrument

That can only be tuned with
Love."

—*Hafiz, from* The Gift

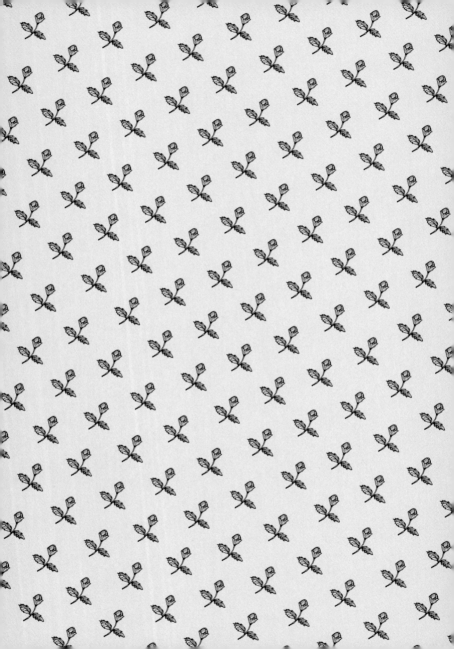

A Special Welcome

"SHALOM! SHALOM!" CRIED MR. MOSEPORE joyfully as he entered the front door to our home, instinctively slipping the brown rubber sandals off his feet so he wouldn't wear down the carpets. Then, with a big smile, the tiny man, who was sporting an oversized suit jacket, embraced Ed's shoulders and kissed him cheek to cheek. I sensed the admiration, respect, and friendship between the two men ran deep.

Ed introduced Mr. Mosepore as a professor of philosophy at the University of Isfahan, and Nancy's and his good friend. At first glance, it was hard to believe Mr. Mosepore was a man of such a respectable position, but his worldly wisdom soon revealed itself though his outspoken manner and candid words. Virtually no subject was off-limits—religion, politics, money, marriage, and sex were all topics of conversation. Mr. Mosepore was filled with curiosity, knowledge, and thought on nearly every topic. And, to my surprise, his lively conversations weren't much different from what I'd heard among my family and friends in the United States. Mr. Mosepore's kindness was transparent. You could see it in his eyes and feel it in his presence. His openness was unexpectedly refreshing.

Ed admired Mr. Mosepore's knowledge of Iranian history, culture, and ancient art. Mr. Mosepore admired Ed's knowledge of modern electronics. Seeing they each had something of interest to share as friends, despite all their cultural differences, was not only comforting but deeply inspiring, too.

Many people believe they need to have all things in common with their friends. Sometimes, though, it's the differences in others we need to learn to appreciate for our spirits to grow. How boring this world would be if all people had the same interests or lived exactly the same way of life. We would have no reason to ponder life's mysteries or learn to value the diversity in life. We would have no reason to breathe in new light.

I choose my friends because of what is in their hearts and I hope we can learn from each other, how to live in harmony with our differences. Maybe, someday, Iran, the mystical world, and America, the technical world, will find this harmony.

Just imagine how much safer our world would be if we all understood the true meaning of friendship. Just imagine if we respected and accepted the spirits and cultures of others for what they are. Just imagine how much America could learn from the Iranian's ancient mysticism and how much Iran could learn from our modern technology. Just imagine the possibilities if this peace and harmony would ever come to be. Maybe, someday, we will all realize this acceptance and love for one another is the true meaning of God and Allah's light. This friendship is the true glory of life.

THE ROSES

F OLLOWING THE 45-YEAR-OLD MAN was his wife, who towered
over him by several inches. She was of somber face and medi-
um build, a twenty-two-year-old woman, young enough to be
Mr. Mosepore's daughter. The young woman was shrouded in a
solid black chador, with an elegant black-lace scarf draped over
her face. In her arms, she cradled a hand-woven, wool tribal
purse, filled with scarlet red roses.

"Welcome! Welcome! Welcome to our country!" Mr. Mosepore repeated to Vance, Damon, and me in broken English,
"Welcome to Iran!"

His wife, standing at his side, seemed to be holding back a
smile as she nodded her head in agreement. Mr. Mosepore carried
on as if Vance, Damon, and I were old family friends, whom he
hadn't seen in years. He seemed as happy as Ed and Nancy were
to see us in his country.

Mr. Mosepore handed Vance and Damon each a colorful
woven Bakhtiyar tribal bracelet which, traditionally, were meant
to be wore on the arm, above the elbow. Mr. Mosepore then
motioned for his wife to hand me the bag filled with roses,
explaining that giving flowers and gifts was customary when welcoming others to their country. Smiling, not quite sure what to
say or how to respond, I nodded and said, "Thank you, thank
you so much for the beautiful roses." I sincerely appreciated their

gracious gesture, yet felt a little awkward that I had nothing to give them in return.

Sometimes thank you is all we need to say to others for their generosity. We may feel a little uncomfortable that we have nothing to give in return, but to accept a gift from the heart with joy and sincere appreciation is all the gift giver expects to receive. And these gifts don't always need to be material things. Gifts can be bits and pieces from the heart—a warm smile, a tender touch, a kind word, or a loving thought.

Whatever the gift may be, an object or a word of inspiration, give it with a happy spirit. Receive it with a happy spirit. But, most of all, give simply to give because it comes from your heart.

ZHORI

INTERMITTENTLY PUFFING ON HIS huge cigar, Mr. Mosepore proudly explained to us that Zhori, his wife of two weeks, was a princess of the Bakhtiyar tribe. The Bakhtiyars' were Shiite Muslims, although some of their beliefs were based on one of the world's oldest religions, the ancient faith of Zoroastrianism, whose religious birth began on Persian soil over twenty-five hundred years earlier by a holy man name Zoroaster. Zoroastrianism was the seed from which Persian culture sprung forth and was thought to be the first faith to believe in only one god.

Zoroastrians believed in life after death and taught the final triumph of good over evil. Their concept of a savior and devil, heaven and hell, a judgment day, the resurrection, an afterlife, angels, and even the belief in a halo all had an inherent influence on Judaism, Christianity, and Islamic doctrines. Although Zoroaster predated Christ nearly six centuries and Muhammad roughly twelve hundred years, I was unaware of the powerful impact he had on many of the world's religions until that day.

Zoroastrians worshiped earth, water, and fire. They believed light was the mark of a good and all-powerful God. To Zoroastrians, fire was the symbol of light. In fire temples—their places of worship—a flame of fire was kept continually burning, night and day. In the city of Yazd, Iran, the historical center of the faith, a solitary flame of fire in one temple has been kept burning continually for more than fifteen centuries.

Even the classic design of paisley, printed on textile and woven into Persian carpets, originated from the Zoroastrian faith. The unique design—a flame of fire—was created by Zoroastrians to symbolize their belief in God's light.

The idea of light in connection with God was rooted in Zoroastrianism. Zoroaster taught that God was like light—all light. This was not unlike Moses, who saw God as light in the burning bush, and Christians, who later believed God was the light of love, and kindness—followed by Muslims, who declared God the light of Heaven and Earth.

I thought—how fasinating that in each of the world's key religions whose doctrine was based on only one God, the prophet went on to portray God in the form of light. Each faith sharing this simple and, yet, most fundamental belief of all—that God is light.

After Mr. Mosepore explained some of the Zoroastrian beliefs to us, it became clear that Zoroastrianism had inspired many Judeo-Christian and Islamic ideas, and that Zoroaster's teachings were as essential as other prophet's ideas in forming many of the religious thoughts of our time.

Zoroastrian ideas still lingered in much of the Iranian culture with many of Iran's traditional holidays originating from the faith. Even though the followers had been reduced to a tiny fraction of Iran's population, Zoroastrians were still respected by most Muslims, and their religion was considered as much a part of Iran's culture as Islam, even though they didn't follow the Islamic doctrine.

In the summer, the Bakhtiyars migrated to the green pastures in the mountains west of Isfahan. Mr. Mosepore promised that, come summer, we would all go to the mountains with him and Zhori for a few weeks to experience the Bakhtiyars' nomadic way of life. The history of the Zoroastrian faith and the Bakhtiyar tribe fascinated me, and I looked forward to the trip.

Mr. Mosepore went on to tell us the story of Zhori's father, a king of the nomadic tribe, who had recently died. Zhori was devastated by her father's death; she would go into fits, pulling at her hair and clothes, and banging her head against the wall. Then, she would stop and sob uncontrollably for hours. Zhori decided the only way to take the pain away was to commit suicide, so she could be with her father. Mr. Mosepore said the dramatic scene Zhori displayed was often part of the grieving process among Iranian women and was somewhat expected, especially if the deceased were a close relative or the death unexpected. Displays of grief, even among men, weren't considered disgraceful or weak in the Iranian culture. Instead, such displays were considered an honest expression of pain and sorrow.

Mr. Mosepore explained that Zhori was a student at the university where he taught and her father had been a good friend of his. Mr. Mosepore said he didn't want Zhori to die, so he asked her to marry him. He told Zhori if she wasn't happy in the marriage after six months, she could divorce him or commit suicide, whatever she chose to do was okay with him. After some persuading, Zhori agreed to Mr. Mosepore's untraditional request for marriage.

Marriages were usually arranged in the Iranian society by the parents of the bride and groom. Typically, couples were introduced to each other through family members or friends. The belief was if the man and woman weren't instantly attracted to each other, their love and affection would grow over time. Only a small percentage of Iranian couples actually married out of true love.

Mr. Mosepore said he'd asked Zhori that morning how she liked her life with him as her husband so far. Mr. Mosepore smiled at us, obviously happy. He shrugged his shoulders, looking bashful, and said, "She say she like it and she very happy. I pleased I make her happy."

So, the reason Zhori was somber and dressed all in black wasn't because she was unhappy, but because she was still in mourning for her father's death, with ten of the traditional forty days still to go. During those forty days, it was customary for Iranian women to wear a somber face in public and dress all in black out of respect for the dead. The forty-day-period was believed to give them the necessary time to deal with their grief, but it wasn't unusual for the mourning to continue on for a year. And a widow sometimes opted to wear black for the remainder of her life.

Considering the circumstances, I couldn't help but respect Mr. and Mrs. Mosepore for graciously taking time away from their family to ensure we had a proper welcome on our first day in their country.

At times, love hurts, this is part of love's cycle. The loss of a loved one, whether through death or divorce, can shake our soul, leaving it hollow, with nothing to fill the emptiness inside. We may yearn to be near our loved one, to feel and touch them, yet there's nothing left to hold onto but memories when we need their presence the most. We miss them so deeply in our hearts, we don't know how to continue on without them. We don't know where to go. We

sink into ourselves to find a place that will help heal our soul. We grasp at anything to help take the pain away. We forget this pain is the price we sometimes have to pay for loving. This is part of love's cycle, and when the loved one is gone, the physical cycle of love is complete, but the spiritual love lives on.

A friend once said to me, "My wife wants a divorce, but I don't. I still love her." I replied, "And that's okay. You probably always will love her."

Sometimes when we loss a loved one, whether through death or divorce, we believe we have to stop loving them to take our pain away, but we don't. Life will carry on. We will somehow find a way to live with the pain, and in time the pain will fade, but we never have to stop loving.

If you lose a loved one, learn to say, as Zhori did, "okay" to love. Learn to say "okay" to life. Love all you need to love and live all you need to live. Don't just exist, live! Live life to the fullest. Love until the cycle is complete. If need be, love until it hurts.

DINNER AT MR. MOSEPORE'S HOME

THE NEXT EVENING WE ALL PILED in the little green Jeep and Ed drove us across town to Mr. Mosepore's house for dinner. Mr. Mosepore greeted us at his front door, a cloud of smoke from his cigar filling the room behind him. Throwing his arms into the air, he cheerfully shouted "Shalom! Shalom! Welcome to my home!" Then stepping aside, he motioned for us to enter. One by one, we all followed Ed's lead and respectfully removed our shoes at the door entrance.

A strong scent of rose water defused the smell of cigar smoke that lingered in the air throughout the house. A beautiful red Persian carpet detailed in multifloral patterns covered the center of the living room floor. Along one side of the room were stuffed pillows made of Persian saddlebags. This *poshti* was unique, but similar to the Afghani one we had at home. The room was dim and simply decorated, with only the basic necessities and a few antique pieces of Persian art sparsely scattered about.

In the center of the carpet, several candles flickered amidst a feast of food, which included a salad, garnished with curds of goat cheese, and a platter of fried onions. Additional food was placed in well-used clay bowls, and old metal pots and pans. Saffron rice still steamed in a rice cooker for the lamb kabobs we would eat for dinner, and a pile of flat, round bread was stacked on a white cloth at each end of the carpet.

I didn't count how many people were there, but it looked like several dozen. Mr. Mosepore seemed to have invited most of his family to dinner, including a few cousins. They all smiled and gawked at us, as if we were some kind of entertainment. The communication was awkward and, for the most part, ungainly, because Mr. Mosepore was the only one in his household who spoke English.

We took our places, sitting around the carpet Indian style. Mr. Mosepore's family squatted oddly. I watched closely as his family began to dish up their food, using only bread as their utensil. I felt a little uncivilized, as if I had no manners eating my food without silverware, yet I had no other choice but to follow the example of Mr. Mosepore's family and use my bread too. Mr. Mosepore noticed my struggle. He got up from the floor, went to the kitchen, and came back with chopsticks, as if he thought they would make eating my dinner easier. They didn't. I returned to scooping up the rice and meat with my bread, and then guiding it to my mouth, all along wondering—what on Earth is an Iranian doing with chopsticks in his house.

Except for the crumbles of yucky goat cheese on my plate, I managed to finish my meal. I fumbled a lot and was a little clumsy, but at least I got the odd blend of food inside my stomach instead of on the fancy red carpet.

We don't always need to be so sophisticated, and more often than not, the situation doesn't even call for it. Most situations only call for us to do the best we can with what we've learned in the past or are presently learning.

We may find ourselves in a state of not knowing how to do something or what to do next. This state of not knowing is a natural part of the learning process. This is what we all need to go through before we learn a lesson or before we know what we need to know. At first, we may feel uncomfortable or awkward, or be a little clumsy as we fumble through the lesson. But that's okay, because before we can learn the lesson we first have to go through the experience. And isn't that what life is all about—the lessons, the growth, the wisdom we learn and carry from one day to the next as our journey through life unfolds?

The Shah's Revenge

M Y STOMACH BEGAN TO CHURN as we sat around the carpet, visiting and drinking spice tea flavored with sugar lumps after dinner. I excused myself to use the bathroom, barely getting to the Farsi toilet in Mr. Mosepore's tiny cramped bathroom in time. *This is it!* I thought. This is the Shah's Revenge that Ed had jokingly warned us about getting from the food and water we ate our first few days in Iran.

My stomach felt as if it were going to burst from the pressure. After twenty minutes or so I thought it might be safe to move from my perch. Once again I found myself looking for toilet paper, this time searching desperately, but none could be found. I felt humiliated at this predicament, because I realized this time I couldn't just drip-dry as before. I had no alternative but to use my hands, and then rinse them in cold water from the green garden water pot next to the spigot by the toilet. I promised myself, from that moment on, I would carry tissue in my pocket whenever I left the house.

I later learned from Ed that Mr. Mosepore had toilet paper in a cupboard down the hall. It just wasn't used that often.

My first Iranian dinner was a little more traditional than I believed necessary at the time. But, I did learn that

some things I thought were necessities in my life really weren't necessities at all. They were just things, things I'd never thought of living without.

How many everyday things do you take for granted? How many things have you never thought of living without? Maybe the electricity, a phone, a mirror, or maybe even toilet paper and silverware. Yes, these things make life simpler but, in the realm of it all, they really aren't necessities at all.

I believe the real necessities in life are: the food we eat—not only food for our bodies, but food that comes from a pure heart and fills our spirits with peace, water we drink—not only water to quench our thirst, but water that fills our hearts with compassion and joy, shelter—not only to keep our bodies warm, but a human shelter that protects and trusts, giving us security, human dignity, and hope, and the air we breathe—not only the air we breathe in and out, but also, the air all around us that fills our spirits with love. These are the real necessities in life—feeding our mind, body, and spirit.

So the next time you eat dinner, try setting aside the silverware and use the bread instead. In the realm of it all you, too, can reflect on what you believe the real necessities in life are.

Zhori's Light Heart

W<small>E SAW</small> Z<small>HORI IN AN ENTIRELY</small> different light in the comfort of her own home. She seemed to have two sides—her public life and her private life. Her black attire was gone, replaced with baggy trousers and a loose, white long-sleeved blouse. Her somber face had disappeared, replaced by a soft, kind smile that made her large brown eyes sparkle in innocence. She was playful, fun loving, and off-the-wall, sometimes giggling uncontrollably at life and her husband. Her spirit seemed to have come to life overnight.

Zhori loved to pick up Mr. Mosepore and squeeze him in a tight bear hug, while his feet dangled off the floor. Like a little girl playing a game, Zhori would giggle and tease her husband, because she thought it was so funny he was so small that she could actually pick him up off the ground.

Mr. Mosepore enjoyed Zhori's silly, light-hearted manner. He said this made him feel young and alive, and he knew, without a doubt, she loved and appreciated him, despite his size.

Be silly, lighthearted, and do fun, off-the-wall things that bring out the kid in you. We don't always have to be so somber. Life doesn't always have to be so serious. And we

don't always have to be so proper and stiff. Lighten up! Release your true spirit. Be playful and enjoy being exactly who you are. Relax! Enjoy your life. Have fun with it. This is the only life you have. And, in the process, lift someone's spirit by letting that person know how much he or she is appreciated, accepted, and loved.

PART FIVE

Life in Isfahan

I picked one rose in a hurry.
I was afraid of the Gardner.
Then I heard the soft voice of Him,
"What's the value of one rose?
I give you the whole garden."

—*Rumi, twelfth-century*
mystic Persian poet

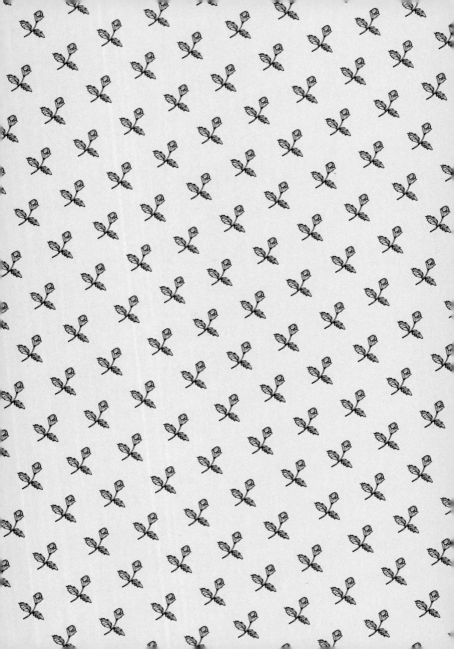

LIFE'S EVERYDAY ROUTINE

OVER THE NEXT FEW MONTHS, our lives settled into an everyday routine. Evenings began with Ed's delicious dinners. Ed loved to cook and we loved his cooking—it was like having a gourmet chef in the house. As a family, though, we often took a stroll down Hafez Street to a classic Iranian restaurant. The eatery doors were always wide open, allowing the aroma and the smoke from grilled meat to filter out in to the street. The quaint little restaurant was furnished with metal tables and chairs, covered in white cloths, and decorated with candles and artificial red roses. We usually ordered lamb kabobs with rice, the traditional Iranian dinner but, if we were desperate for western cooking, we'd try the Iranian version of a Mexican burrito or an American hamburger. Although we often spent more time trying to keep cool under the wobbly ceiling fans, while swatting flies off our plates, than eating the food. Nonetheless, we always felt welcome eating in this restaurant.

After dinner, we often strolled around town, shopping or people watching. The guys occasionally rode Kurt's dirt bikes or drove the Jeep up to the Desert Flats, where they'd race around, horse—playing in the dunes. After the dust settled from all the activity, you could stand on top of the flats and view the whole city of Isfahan sprawled out against the desert. Many evenings, though, we simply lounged around the house, munching on traditional

Iranian snacks, such as pumpkinseeds, popcorn, pomegranates, or pistachio nuts, while visiting with family friends, doing homework, or watching black-and-white reruns of old American TV shows.

In Iran, the telephone wasn't used to chat with friends and family as much as in the United States because dialing out could be frustrating. Phone lines were often full, with a busy signal replacing the dial tone. We felt quite lucky if we made a connection or got through an entire phone conversation without being accidentally cut off or interrupted by one of our many party lines. Most calls we received were from Farsi-speaking Iranians who had dialed the wrong number or had been incorrectly connected by the shoddy phone system. The caller often babbled on for a few minutes, as if we were suppose to understand everything they said. Then, in the middle of a sentence, they would get frustrated because we didn't understand them, and then simply hang up, leaving whoever picked up the phone baffled as to what had been said.

Days began at the wake-up call from the *Muezzin* calling the faithful to prayer. Mornings were filled with the rush of preparing for the day ahead. After we each showered, we sat on the *poshti* and ate breakfast, which consisted of one little bottle of milk poured over a bowl of imitation Farsi Rice Krispies or Corn Flakes. An old peasant man from the village sometimes delivered the milk door-to-door. The man crept down the *koche* with his donkey, its bells jingling as it pulled an overloaded cart filled with crates of milk. Neither the milk nor the cereal tasted quite the same as in the States. Yet, we didn't have much of a choice but to eat them and, over time, we actually grew to like them. Although I never let down my guard while eating the cereal, always paying close attention to the ingredients, which occasionally included pebbles or little worm-like weevils. The pebbles I ignored, but if I saw a worm floating in the milk, I immediately placed my hands over my mouth and then hurried to the bathroom to get rid of what I'd already eaten.

After breakfast, we rushed to the school bus waiting at the end of the *koche*. Then we headed out into the morning sunrise for the long forty-five-minute ride across the purple desert to Toufanian High School, the American School of Isfahan. In the far distance we could see pale lavender mountains and ancient gray pigeon towers standing motionless against the sky. And, as we passed by villages that bordered the dusty roads, we could see peasants carrying on their daily lives, just as their ancestors had for thousands of years.

Despite the country's prosperity from oil profits, not much money seemed to go to the simple needs of the poor. This was visible each day as I looked out the bus window to see chador-covered women, squatting in the sand next to their crumbling mud dwellings, mixing bread in old clay bowls, and cooking over hot stones and open flames fueled by dung. Electricity and phones were still out of reach for most villages, even though they weren't far from town. Despite the lack of modern resources, most peasants seemed perfectly content living off the natural wonders of the land.

Poverty was the only way of life many Iranians had ever known, although many of the poor didn't even seem to fathom what poverty was. Usually born into peasant families, they lived out their days in rural villages or dilapidated mud houses in town. What appeared to keep them struggling on each day was their undying faith in God, which seemed to give them their whole sense of purpose in life. The peasants were often naive to the ways of the modern world, which, at times, made me almost too aware of my western upbringing. These were simple, yet complex, people, often more appreciative of respect and a kind heart than of money. At times, I felt uncomfortable, out of place, and somewhat tainted around them, as if I were too modern, too painted, and too educated, yet naive of the Iranian's ancient civilization and all its wisdom. Their innocence of the modern world and their deep connection to nature seemed nearer to God's truth than my own civilization.

As if frozen in time since the biblical era, village men still roamed the desert dressed in heavy woolen clothes, with caps or turbans protecting their heads from the parching heat. The only visible sign of the twentieth century was the occasional sighting of a peasant man wearing worn-out, white Adidias sneakers with no laces. With a donkey at their sides and the support of a walking stick, the men herded their flocks of sheep down lonely, dusty roads that crisscrossed through the desert.

Long ago abandoned ruins stood knee-deep in sand drifts, and every so often we'd see a pack of famished dogs running wild through the desert, scavenging for food and water in the dry heat. *Joob* dogs and cats were considered rodents to most Iranians and few had them as pets. Those who did were usually Christians or Armenians. The wild dogs were hunted in the desert, typically once a year, to thin the packs.

Although bicycles were no ten speeds, some of the villagers were lucky enough to have old-fashioned bikes to pedal to town—that is if they made it to town. Evidence that some didn't was clearly visible, with many abandoned bicycles lying rusted and broken down on the desert beside the road. Old jalopies often raced past the school bus, whirling up dust clouds that blinded our driver. The cars easily left us behind in the thick powder as they continued down the road, going well over the posted speed limit of 120 kilometers an hour. Sometimes the vehicles were jam-packed with what must have been entire villages crammed into one automobile, with heads, arms, and legs sticking out windows and, occasionally, even from the trunk. I never understood if the Iranians crammed the cars full of people out of necessity or if they were restless and bored, and they needed something to do—anything to break the pattern of the humdrum life they lived.

Despite my western upbringing, I managed to adjust to all the cultural peculiarities around me. They subtly became an ordinary part of our everyday way of life in Isfahan.

Routine is an essential part of our lives. It keeps us balanced, on time, and centered. The simple things we do help our lives move forward, on course, into the future. Sometimes we even get caught up in the security that comes from each day being a repeat of yesterday. Nothing seems right when we break the pattern. We feel we're walking out of beat, life seems off balance. But, after a while, we may become restless and bored with the life we're living. A humdrum routine sets in—nothing seems to inspire us. We're caught in a vicious circle, like whirling dust clouds blinding us to what we're missing.

Maybe when we feel this humdrum life set in, it's time to break the routine and do something spontaneous that throws us off balance. Maybe it's time to kick off our shoes, stick our legs out the window, or simply let the breeze blow on our face. Knowing that it's okay to lose track of time, it's okay to lose our balance. Because, sometimes, that's what it takes to get us back on our feet and centered again.

Toufanian High School

Toufanian High School, the American School of Isfahan, was located near the American compound. The school was built in the middle of nowhere, surrounded by a high, chain-link fence and secured by armed guards patrolling the other side. The grounds looked more like a prison than a school, but the atmosphere was the same as any traditional high school in America. Besides a few foreigners, students were a blend of teenagers from all over the United States. But, no matter what background we came from—the flashy lights of New York City, the tropical beaches of Florida, the barren deserts of Arizona, or the green valleys of Oregon—we all had one common bond—experiencing the world we were in together, a world so different from our own. We didn't talk much about our life in Iran. We didn't need to. We knew what we were experiencing was real and, at times, the words to describe the world around us were simply too hard to find.

Even though Toufanian High School provided an excellent education by some of the finest teachers from America and Great Britain, it didn't offer the cultural lessons needed to help the students understand the Iranians and their way of life. Our wisdom came from the Iranians themselves. At school, it was as if the world outside the chain-link fence didn't exit.

School days ended with the long bus ride back to Isfahan. During this time I'd often watch out the window in silence, taking in the desert life. Even though sometimes there was nothing that could be seen, except for tumbleweeds and desert sand being whisked up by a light wind, and then whirled up into the air, only to be cast back in to the middle of the flat, barren wasteland. The same wasteland where many say the cradle of civilization was born.

Isn't it refreshing to know that others have experienced similar events in their life? We can appreciate and understand what others have been through or are going through because we've been there, or are going through it, too. We don't always have to talk about it and, sometimes, nothing valid can be said. Nothing can explain the thoughts or emotions tumbling through our heads. Sometimes the words to express what we've seen or felt can't be found. But, even without words, experiences can create common bonds that tie hearts together. Sometimes just being near others in an inexpressible situation validates our circumstances and gives us a comfort we can't explain.

Sometimes we simply need to take the time to sort through the experience. The words will come to us when we begin to understand the lesson but, sometimes, it takes a while, maybe even years, before we comprehend what we've learned. So don't think you need to grasp the understanding of an experience at the moment it happens. The insight will come to you and, someday, you'll see the wisdom placed in your heart from the lesson.

The Roads

Vance bought a beat-up, white '65 Volkswagen for $300. The car wasn't much to look at, but at least it ran, gave us some independence, and relieved Ed and Nancy from chauffeuring us around town. The VW spit and sputtered as we cruised around the city streets.

The streets were lined with a hodgepodge of shops: garment dealers, carpet merchants, teahouses, bread makers, and candy, herb, spice, and trinket shops. Many vendors sold their goods from primitive stucco and brick buildings located behind tall, slender, poplar-like trees that bordered the sidewalks.

City thoroughfares were crowded with pedestrians, donkey carts, bicyclists, mopedders, and an odd assortment of other methods of transportation, each trying to dodge the other. Given that, we quickly learned the rules of the road, which were fairly simple: the bigger car had the right of way and trucks unconditionally had the right of way. Intersections could be rather confusing, though, since green lights were considered red if a truck was passing through them. Two-way streets easily became one-way or one-way streets became two-way, depending on which way rush-hour traffic started to flow. If you missed your turn— no problem—just make a U-turn in the middle of the road or simply back up. And speed, in spite of the traffic laws, was out of control. We promptly learned to respect the power of size, as well as the importance of good horns and brakes.

The city's spirited pace never seemed to end, consequently little fender-benders were a natural part of the scenery. Hardly any car, new or old, was without its battle wounds, consisting of small and large dents, dings, or scratches. People involved in an accident would stop their cars in the middle of the road, (that's if the accident hadn't) and then jump out, yelling and waving their hands in the air, blaming each other for the incident. Meanwhile, people stalled in the traffic jam that abruptly formed behind them, hung their heads out the window, impatiently trying to resolve the situation by waving their hands, honking their horns, and shouting at the victims to move out of the way—as if all the commotion they were creating was actually going to speed up the process.

The only ones who seemed to benefit from accidents were the pedestrians, bicyclists, and mopedders. They took advantage of the situation by safely darting in and out between the stalled traffic.

If such a thing as car insurance existed in Iran, it never seemed to come into play. Because after all was said and done, the people involved in an accident would calm down, turn around, and walk off, still shaking their heads as they climbed back in their cars and drove away. Their frustrations were vented, the incident concluded, and soon, all was forgotten.

It's okay to say what's on your mind. You don't always have to hold it in. We should try to be polite and courteous at all times. But, sometimes, these ways block our true emotions, our true passion, our true thoughts and

feelings, *making us become uptight, resentful, and bitter.*

Wouldn't life with others be much simpler if the road that led from one person to another was clear, with no traffic inbetween? Wouldn't it be a relief if we could say what's on our mind and take care of our thoughts, feelings, and emotions, this clearing a path to forgiveness and peace? Maybe we should stop in our path and take care of the situation at the moment it happens and not let it weigh on our shoulders or stew in our minds. Perhaps getting our frustrations out is best; conclude the incident and honestly clear our thoughts and feelings for the road ahead.

Ask yourself, "Have I done all I can to resolve the situations in my life? Have I truly forgiven others or is an incident still lingering in the back of my mind? Is traffic still blocking the road that leads from my soul to another?" If this is so, maybe it's time to let go of the pride that prevents you from saying what's really on your mind. Perhaps it's time to feel your true emotions, to express your true thoughts, to clear your conscience, and to let others know where you stand. Then, if need be, calm down, turn around, and walk away, knowing you've done and said all you can at that moment to take care of yourself and the situation. Shake your head. Let peace come to you as you begin down the road to forgiveness.

THE GRAND BAZAAR

L IKE SPOKES ON A WHEEL, the city streets of Isfahan always ended in the hub of Shah's Square. If we happened to get lost, we simply looped around and followed the streets back to the center of Shah's Square. In the heart of the plaza, a huge park overflowed with fountains and rose gardens. A one-way stone road bordered the park, which had once served as a polo arena and a stage for Persian entertainment, where preachers, poets, storytellers, jugglers, and magicians all amused the crowds.

The climax of Shah's Square was in the sixteenth century, during the reign of Abbas I, the Great Shah of Iran. The Shah built the city center into a stunning historical landscape of palaces, mosques, and gardens. Throughout the Islamic world, the Shah was infamous for throwing scandalous parties, pampering his guests with the pleasure of fine wines produced from grapes grown in Persian soil. The ancient goal post still stood in what used to be the polo field. Other than that, all the old ways of entertaining had long since disappeared, except for an occasional magician wandering through the crowds.

The Royal Mosque and the tall minarets at the south end of Shah's Square, and the Grand Bazaar at the north end—only a few blocks from our house—were always alive and thriving with foreign tourists and ordinary townspeople who patronized the historical plaza. The bazaar was the main marketplace and the heart of activity in the Iranian community. This was a common gathering place for beggars, peddlers, swindlers, and shoppers. The religious and political livelihood was dependent on the marketplace's prosperity and spirit. The only day the bazaar lay silent was Friday, the Muslims' holy day of prayer.

Weekends were a time for us to discover the ancient nooks and crannies in the Grand Bazaar. The bazaar was built of primitive, arch-covered tunnels, made of stucco and brick with high-beamed ceilings, where uneven swags of bare light bulbs hung from tattered cords. Beneath the lights stood mazes of dimly lit crisscrossed alleys that continued intertwining for miles. The narrow alleys were filled with small booths, behind which merchants sold their wares. Each shop had its own unique merchandise. Echoes from the famous Isfahan block printers, stamping paisley and mythical designs on unbleached cloth for tapestries and garments they created, gave rhythm to the bazaar's life. Persian carpet dealers stacked their colorful carpets in piles or proudly hung them from wires with the fringe brushing the ground below. Fine handcrafted jewelry from the gold and silversmiths twinkled through dust-covered glass cases, brightening up the merchants' booths as we passed by.

The sprawling marketplace was filled with hundreds of other shops such as shoe vendors, pottery makers, leather crafts, and fabric, spice, herb, and trinket shops. Yet all the bazaar merchants had one thing in common. They loved to see foreigners browsing around and they often competed for our attention by haggling, conning, smiling, and charming us as they motioned for us to step into their shops. More often than not, though, we continued through the alleys, passing booth after booth.

Dust stirred from the crowds as feet beat on the uneven, hard, dirt-covered ground. The dust created a haze through which I could smell the aroma of incense, spices, tobacco, tea, and opium pipe smoke drift through the air, tickling my nose and confusing my senses. I often watched old men who seemed perfectly content squatting in their stalls, listening to soothing Persian music, and heating the bottom of their opium pipe bowls as they puffed on their long-stemmed pipes. Opium was legal in Iran for elderly men because it helped ease the pain of natural diseases that often accompany old age, giving the men more comfort and pleasure in their last years of life.

Nearly whatever we needed or wanted could be found in the Grand Bazaar. The marketplace was no K-Mart—nothing had a set price. The merchandise was all bought through a gift of wheeling, dealing, and negotiating with the shopkeeper to get a fair price. Sometimes, we spent hours or even days of haggling before we walked away with our prized possession, which often made us think twice about our purchase and whether the time spent bickering with the shopkeeper was worth the price.

I often wonder if we all had to go through the experience of wheeling and dealing to make a purchase in America how clean our closets, our conscience and our Mother Earth would be.

Maybe we should all walk away from the things we believe we must have and take time to seriously think through our needs. Knowing we are doing this, not only for our own conscience but, for the sake of our Mother Earth and our children's future.

So think twice about each purchase you make. Is what

*you have your eyes on now something you genuinely
want? Is it something you truly need? Or, is it something
you might forget about once it's out of sight?*

*Step away for a moment, an hour, a day, or a week.
Chances are what you had your eyes on will be right
where you last saw it, if you find it's something you genuinely want or truly need. If not, then maybe there's a
deeper reason it wasn't meant to be.*

LIGHT IN THE TUNNELS

FINDING OUR WAY OUT OF the Grand Bazaar could sometimes be a challenge, depending on how deep we ventured into the maze of tunnels. We'd been told that if we took the wrong route, the tunnels would eventually vanish into private courtyards or gardens of small palaces located at the far end of the marketplace. But, somehow, we always managed to find the right way out, by weaving in and out of the crisscrossed alleys until a faint glimpse of light emerged at the end of a passageway. Then, recognizing familiar booths along the way, we'd work our way toward the light until, little by little, the light became brighter and brighter through the dusty haze. At last, narrowing our eyes to daylight, we'd step out of the bazaar's cave-like entrance into a warm burst of sun rays penetrating Shah's Square.

Many of us find ourselves weaving though life, trying to see a glimpse of light at the end of a tunnel. But sometimes the light is so faint; we can only detect it in the eye of our soul as we try to find our way out of a particular relationship or place.

At times we seem to be going nowhere but around in a hopeless maze of confusion, seemingly nowhere near the light. But as we begin to work through the circumstances in our lives, that tiny glimpse of light inside of us begins to glow and urge us forward. Step by step, we follow it. We continue on until, suddenly, the way feels right—no more dead-ends. The light becomes brighter and brighter, and it becomes much more intense until, finally, we find our way out. "Yes," we say, "I've gone the right way." Then we may ask ourselves, "But why didn't I go that way before? Why did I get stuck in the maze?" And then the insight becomes clear. That was the lesson. The light was always there. We simply need to be patient and follow that tiny glimpse of light within us. Then we'll find our way out, through the comfort of clarity that lights up our soul.

The Copper Teakettle

EACH TIME VANCE AND I VISITED the Grand Bazaar, we took a stroll down Copper Alley located outside the bazaar entrance. We could see and hear craftsmen hammering and pounding their wares into shape and form. Copper and brass pots and pans were suspended in the air, clinking and clanking together in the breeze like wind chimes echoing as they dance through the air.

Delighted to see an American admiring his wares, the sun-weathered shopkeeper—dressed in his best suit jacket, polyester pants, and rubber sandals—would present his toothless smile, ready to deal a bargain while proclaiming his price and goods were the best. Rubbing the course stubble on his face, he would name some ridiculous price for his goods, and then try to read the reaction on our faces. The shopkeeper's main purpose in life seemed to be getting top dollar for his wares, especially from foreign tourists he could see coming for blocks, with expensive cameras slung over their shoulders and sporting trendy visor caps, posh sunglasses, and Bermuda shorts. The shopkeeper often had his elder son at his side, who was more than eager to learn and carry on his father's ways of bargaining for his trade.

But it was a giant, hammered copper teakettle I had my eye on that always brought us back to Copper Alley. The teakettle was so huge it made me laugh, yet it was so charming and full of character it made me smile and wish Vance and I could buy it.

The teakettle's polished orange glow brought warmth to my eyes as it reflected my face like a mirror.

Someday Vance and I would return to buy the copper teakettle, when our negotiating skills were a little more refined. Maybe then we could get the shopkeeper to reduce his price. So we always made our way back through Copper Alley to test our bargaining skills and to ensure the teakettle was still there where we last saw it.

Sometimes an object catches my eye—something about it warms my spirit. Most of us have these special objects around us that bring warmth to our souls. It may be a painting, a family heirloom, or a special chair. Whatever the object may be, it just sits there and talks to us, but we can't hear it because it speaks softly to our eyes.

Objects add color to our world. We sometimes look at them because of the way they silently touch our spirit and bring delight or inspiration to our eyes. You know these objects when you see them. They are special only to you. They bring back memories or encourage dreams. They bring out your spirit, what pleases you and what makes you laugh, smile, or cry. They touch your spirit and emotions in ways that sometimes you can't even explain why. The object may be special only in your eyes, but that's what our eyes are for—to help fill our spirit along the way. So, be choosey about the objects you place in your world. Let them have worth in your heart, through your eyes.

A Summer Job

I TOOK A PART-TIME SUMMER JOB babysitting for a nine-year-old American girl named Erica. Erica was bright and independent for her age, so I never thought of myself as a babysitter, just someone to keep her occupied during the long, hot summer days. But, at times, keeping Erica entertained could be quite a challenge so, on those days, we took a taxi to the American Company Activity Center, several miles away from Erica's home. At the center we could swim in the pool or visit with Vance while he worked at the snack bar.

To flag down a taxi, we'd lean from the sidewalk into the street where the cab drivers sped around to find commuters. The proper way to attract a taxi driver's attention was to holler the name of a landmark, such as a thoroughfare or square that was closest to our destination. If the driver were headed that way, he'd stomp on his brakes, and then quickly negotiate a price. If we agreed, he'd nod his head for us to hop into the back seat of his taxi.

One day, Erica and I stepped into the back seat of a cab before I thoroughly checked out the driver. By the time I noticed his messy hair and the fearless look in his eyes through the rear-view mirror, it was already too late. The driver had floored the gas pedal, taking us from 0 to 50 mph in about ten seconds. The force of the speed tugged at our faces and threw us against the back seat. We desperately tried to find something to hold on to as he wildly zipped in and out of the chaotic traffic. Then, with one hand on the steering wheel and the other slung over the back of the front seat, the driver calmly glanced back at me and asked in a mixture of Farsi and English, "*Khahoon* (Madam), where you say go?" Before we knew it, he'd come to a screeching halt at our destination. A little shaken, but still in one piece, we stepped out of the taxi to safety. After that incident, I decided Erica and I were much safer walking to the pool through the unbearable heat, skipping over small scorpions and centipedes that crept along the sidewalks, than taking a chance on accepting another ride from a fearless man behind the steering wheel of a taxi cab.

Early one afternoon, as Erica and I were walking and working our way toward the center, I saw a peculiar old lady who seemed to appear out of nowhere. I watched her—curiously, becoming more disturbed each moment by her appearance. I hadn't witnessed her depth of poverty among the Iranian women before. Her filthy black chador was tattered and torn, lying over her rag garments, skimming the ground beneath her dusty feet. She appeared sick, weak, and tired. A cloud of humiliation and dishonor seemed to follow her as she wandered aimlessly through the blistering streets, her body supported only by a crooked walking stick. Finally, she came to rest on the busy corner of the city park.

Oblivious to the backdrop of the park and its colorful rose garden behind her, she turned, her solid white eyes emotionless as she squatted, wrapped her chador around her, and cast her face to the ground. The only sign left of a living soul beneath the bundled pile was the silent motion as she nodded her head when she felt a coin drop into the palm of her sun-withered hand, stretched out from beneath her chador.

I realized how long I'd been observing the woman when Erica impatiently tugged at my arm, eager to continue down the road to the pool. I fumbled in my purse, trying to find some coins to place in the woman's hand. But all I could find were a few *rials,* just enough money for Erica and me to buy a Coke at the center snack bar. I took Erica's hand, and we turned and walked away.

I struggled to erase the woman from my mind as I relaxed on a lounge chair near the swimming pool. The sun beat down on my back as I watched giant roaches scurry on the ground beneath my chair. No matter how hard I tried to keep occupied though, I couldn't shake the image of the woman from my mind. Although I knew my questions would never be answered, I still wondered where she came from. Where was her family to care for her, or had she been shunned? What was her name? What brought her there? Where was her home? Had she been a carpet weaver, or had she been born deaf and dumb? But it was her poverty of loneliness that bothered me the most. After witnessing her struggle it was as if I could feel her pain inside my heart. Even though this pain wasn't mine, it was so pure, complete, and real.

As I sipped my soda, the image of the woman stood still in the silence of my mind where it tugged at my heart and haunted my conscience with one lingering thought: I could have had water.

Our teachers often appear in our path out of nowhere, and they don't have to be professors, counselors, or priests. These teachers are just people who teach us something special along the way. Sometimes we don't even realize the impact their arrival has on our lives until much later,

after we reflect on the significance of their presence in our lives. Then we understand why they were there, teaching us what we needed to know.

It's like a fairy tale when our teachers arrive at the time they do. It's as if they were meant to be there all along, teaching us, according to our needs. Our teachers may give us a polite gesture or a warm smile, or they may make us laugh or cry when we need it the most. Sometimes they touch our spirits without even realizing the influence they've had on our lives.

I believe the presence of the peasant woman in my life wasn't for the purpose of what I could give her but, rather, what she could give me. I now realize I did drink water—water that flowed from her soul to mine as she filled my heart with a deep, heartfelt understanding of compassion.

No amount of money I placed in the beggar's hand could have been exchanged for what she placed in my heart. Because, in the end, I didn't see a beggar beneath the bundled pile, I saw a soul. A human being with needs just like mine. A person who needed to be loved and understood, a human being at a depth of poverty I'd never seen before, not only poverty of the body, but poverty of the spirit. Yet, with what little strength she had, she kept struggling on. This left me to always wonder what really kept her alive: was it her body, or was it her soul, searching for the compassion and love that can only come from other souls?

THE 'JOOBS'

W E'D OFTEN WALK TO A LITTLE CANDY SHOP on the corner
of Moshir-an-sari to buy old-fashioned rock candy. Or,
sometimes we'd tag along with Ed to purchase milk, vegetables,
herbs, or bread from the vendors on Hafez Street. The bread ven-
dor, dusted from head to toe in flour, continually tossed flat slabs
of dough on top of hot stones for his never-ending stream of cus-
tomers. Some regulars stopped by the shop several times a day to
purchase freshly baked bread for each meal. The flat, round bread
had a pitted, bubbly crust that always needed close inspection
before eating because frequently pebbles were embedded in the
dough from the baking stones.

On our way to and from the food vendors, we'd see Iranian
women carrying bulky buckets full of water, which they drew
from public spigots on the street corners. For those households
without piped-in city water, the water from the spigots was their
only clean water for daily cooking and washing. The poorer
women, mostly from the rural areas, squatted in front of the
public *joobs* filled with cold, murky water. Sometimes the
women squatted there for hours, washing piles of dirty clothes
and dishes. The water was produced from melted snow from the
mountains, and then diverted to the *joobs,* which ran alongside
the streets in the city center. Throughout the centuries, *joobs* had
traditionally been used as the main water source for washing,

111

dumping rubbish, and drinking. Although seeing someone drink from the polluted water was rare, it occasionally still happened.

I'd often pause and watch in bewilderment, as the women washed their belongings in the *joobs,* wondering if I was missing something because none of their actions made sense to me. But, no matter how long or hard I observed I still couldn't see what would make the women believe their garments and dishes would ever get clean in the filthy water running through the ditches. I finally realized that the women's concept of clean simply wasn't the same as mine, and who was I to judge their twenty-five hundred-year-old civilization; after all, I was only seventeen years old.

Sometimes we unconsciously expect other people to act, believe, and see as we do. But we should keep in mind that we can't honestly compare someone else's actions to our own, because we aren't that person and we haven't experienced his or her life.

So if other people's actions aren't harming them or others, then why should they bother us? Maybe it's time to let others be. Free them from our expectation and let them live their lives as they please—in peace.

A Whimsical Way of Life

As I BECAME ACCUSTOMED TO THE whimsical way of Iranian life, the unordinary became ordinary and humor took on a whole different light. Sometimes the activities in the streets were like watching a live comedy, but I was the only audience, trying to understand what I could and couldn't see in this fascinating world around me.

People were going every which way on the streets with no real sense of direction. Cries from vendors only added to the confusion as they yelled from the open doors of their shops, haggling with people to step in and buy their goods. Vehicles were a jumble of new cars and old jalopies—Volkswagens, trucks, buses, taxis, and other strange-looking, foreign cars I'd never seen before. Nearly every vehicle had religious ornaments lying on the dash or hanging from a mirror, and all had a right-side steering wheel.

The peasant men from the villages came to town with nothing but a scraggly donkey and a few sheep tagging behind them. Then, with their donkeys stacked high and weighted down on the sides with saddlebags full of food and supplies, the men would quietly disappear down the street, leaving behind only animal hoof prints and spots of dung on the ground as they wandered back to their villages on the outskirts of town.

It wasn't even unusual to see an Iranian woman's chador fluttering in the breeze behind her as she buzzed around on a moped with a child balanced on the handlebars or in a basket. Only a few Iranians seemed to be prospering from the country's oil-rich economy. The privileged often dressed in trendy, western designer clothes. And cruised around town in shiny imported Mercedes and BMWs, making the gap between the rich and the poor plain to see.

Nonetheless, everyone and everything was welcome in the streets. Even poster-sized pictures of the dead, framed in metal and laced with rose garlands, dotted the sidewalks for the whole community to grieve the loved one's death. These haunting, yet beautiful memorials seemed to say to all those who passed—we are all just brothers and sisters in the end.

I often wondered how the Iranian people could ever completely move forward into the modern world and still hold onto their deep-rooted faith and whimsical way of life. The rise of modernization and western ideals in the Iranian culture were all too certain. Just as in the rest of the world, there was no turning back the clock. But when the transformation of Iran was complete, what would be the real cultural cost?

Treasure life's whimsical ways. We don't always have to know why life is the way it is. We don't always need to wonder and search so hard for a reason or an answer to why things are the way they are. Life doesn't always have to be so crystal clear. The magical answer doesn't always have to be there.

Don't believe you must always see the clarity when life makes no sense to you because, sometimes, the clarity just isn't there. Now and then, we simply need to relish in the surprise of the moment, even though we don't understand its lesson yet. Sometimes we only need to accept what we see and its mystery. The clarity will come if it's meant to. But, for now, remember—we all have our own special purpose in this whimsical world.

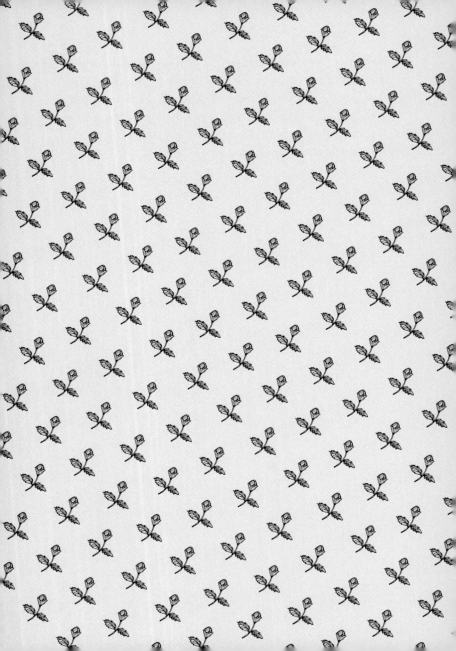

PART SIX

Reflections of Persian Art

The
Difference
Between a good artist
And a great one

Is:

The novice
Will often lay down his tool
Or brush

Then pick up an invisible club
On the mind's table

And helplessly smash the easels and
Jade.

Whereas the vintage man
No longer hurts himself or anyone
And keeps on
Sculpting

Light.

—*Hafiz, from* The Gift

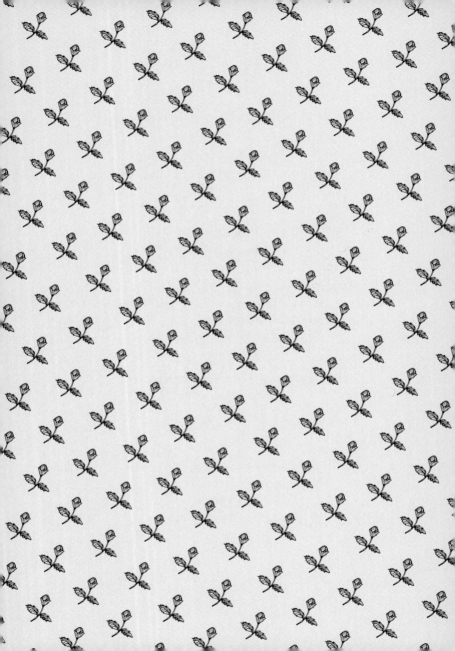

CALLIGRAPHY

PERSIAN ART ALONE TOOK ME into another world, with the ancient art not much different from the modern. When I first arrived in Iran, Farsi handwriting looked like nothing more than ugly scribbles displayed on signs and billboards all around me. But, over time, I began to see the writings differently—for what they were. Within the swirls, dots, and scribbles, my eyes began to see the elegant art of ancient calligraphy.

During the period before printing, calligraphy became a highly refined art. A man's spiritual state and his thought were often reflected in his calligraphy style and writings. Many of the world's great calligraphers arose from the Persian culture, performing a vital role in the early creation of the ancient art.

Calligraphy began in the Islamic world with the Qur'an, originating as a sacred art form to preserve and glorify the holy book, which was often meticulously hand-written in a majestic writing style. The ancient scribbles were visible everywhere in Isfahan, from complex passages written on mosques and minarets, to elaborate lacework carved in stucco or metalwork. But the collection of old Persian verses, gracefully written on hand-decorated paper, are what reflected the magnitude of elegance in all the calligraphy before my eyes. The beauty of calligraphy only intensified once I began to appreciate its passage to antiquity through the deep-rooted world around me.

At times we need to look at a picture from a different perspective. Things aren't always as they first appear. When we begin to understand and value the whole scene, our point-of-view changes and the picture becomes clearer. Deep within the scene, we may see something that wasn't there before, something we couldn't see at first glance.

We may meet a person who we believe is physically unattractive but, over time, we begin to see beneath their physical being—a spirit with a fun-loving nature, and a caring and thoughtful way. We begin to see beauty differently when we see with our hearts and minds—not only with our eyes.

So don't just look at the surface of things, look in depth at the whole picture, including those things that can't be understood. Use more than your eyes to see. Use all your senses, while opening your mind and heart, too. Only then will you see beneath all the ugliness in the world—the magnificent elegance the universe has relinquished to you. Only then will you see true beauty in the world.

INLAID BOXES

I WATCHED IN AMAZEMENT AS TINY, carved pieces of bone, wood, ivory, mother-of-pearl, and stone were intricately inlaid together by skilled Iranian craftsmen who sat in their stalls for hours, creating little patterns like tiny puzzles. The meticulously hand-crafted pieces covered backgammon boards, pipes, tobacco boxes, and framed, daintily detailed miniature pictures, which typically feature ancient Persian men and women posed with mythical animals, musical instruments, vases, or swords. Many of the miniature pictures were carved from or painted on chips of bone.

The slanted eyes painted on the faces in the miniature pictures were a quiet reminder of the Mongol invasion in the thirteenth century, a heritage of which many Iranians were ashamed. The Iranians believed the Mongols had tainted their country when they savagely invaded Persia, slaughtering and starving thousands upon thousands of Persian people and raping Persian women. Every city and village in the Mongols' path was systematically destroyed through their army's massive assault of butchery and terror. They left behind beheaded bodies swimming in pools of blood, and pyramids of Iranian men, women, and children's skulls to be viewed by those few whose lives were spared. The Mongols viciously wiped out most of Persia's history by burning Persian poetry, books, and art in each community they ravaged.

The mysticism of poetry and art was treasured by Persians because it provided a means by which one could surrender all sense of self in the material world to reach unity with God.

The Mongols brutal assault on Persia was not only physical; it was cultural and spiritual too, diminishing a country built on the faith of Zoroastrianism and Islam to bare bones and ashes. Today, the invasion by the Mongols still lives on in the minds and hearts of many Iranian people, cutting through to the very soul of Persian culture, honor, pride, and dignity.

The country of Persia seemed carved and placed together like the intricate, inlaid miniature puzzles created by its people. The country itself seemed composed of the beauty of ivory and mother-of-pearl, the hardness of wood, and the ugliness of bone, which seemed to symbolize its nation's history. All of this created the soul of Iran, a country made constantly on guard and ever mindful of the powerful forces in the outside world.

Some of us wander through life with the ugliness of yesterday controlling our lives and emotions. We may be ashamed or humiliated by events of the past. But if we say the world is full of ugliness, then ugliness is all we will see. If we hold onto those thoughts, bitterness builds and hardens our soul. We begin to believe that's the way life is. But the truth is, we see in life what we want to see.

We can't change the past, but we can move forward into the present, into the moment we now are living. Sometimes, though, to mend our hearts, we must return to the past long enough to heal our souls. And this is fine if that's where we need to go. Because only when we acknowledge the past and accept it can we truly heal and open our hearts to the present. Only then can we trust again and allow the world around us to gently teach us of humility and peace. Only then can we truly surrender our spirit to love.

We don't have to wander through life with the ugliness of the past in our hearts. We don't have to carry the shame or humiliation from our past with us. Feel what you need to feel, and then release any ugliness that lingers in your soul. Remembering the past was the way it had to be for whatever reason, a reason you may never know. Yet, someday, you may see why things had to be the way they were, and how the ugliness and beauty in your life have blended together, creating the beautiful picture painted deep within your soul.

PERSIAN CARPETS

PERSIAN CARPETS MADE OF SILK or wool were carefully hand-tied together with millions of tiny knots, which, when precisely arranged, created beautiful designs of paisley, floral, and animal patterns. Top-quality carpets could be recognized by more knots per square inch and more tightly woven threads. Some carpets had touches of silver and gold silk threads woven into the design, creating an iridescent cast over the elaborate pictures. The use of dyes from fruits, nuts, plants, roots, and vegetables gave Persian carpets natural, rich, vivid colors, such as indigo blues, pomegranate reds, and pistachio greens.

Through the ages, carpets had become a cherished possession in Persian culture. The carpets were used to eat, sit, sleep, and pray on, and often given as gifts. Shoes were removed before stepping onto them, with respect to their uses, heritage, and worth. Each carpet was rich in history and most reflected the weaver's tribe, geographical location, era, or religious belief.

Religion was as diverse in Iran as it is in the west, with Muslims, Jews, Christians, Zoroastrians, and an assortment of other faiths all finding their home in the Persian culture, each creating their own distinctive carpets. Iranian people, despite their religious beliefs, all shared an intense pride in their country regarding their Persian heritage.

One day, as Nancy and I strolled through the carpet market,

she pointed out a young weaver fidgeting with her chador to free her hands, so she could rub her eyes. Nancy said the woman would most likely be able to create only one or two large carpets in her lifetime before she started to lose her sight. Although Nancy had previously told me about elderly carpet weavers going blind, this story never hit me so powerfully as the moment when I saw that young woman possibly weaving her way to a life without sight. That's when I began to appreciate the worth of a Persian carpet and understood why the price was so high.

From the outside world looking in, the story behind each carpet would have taken a lifetime to understand. Because the unique designs and pictures woven into the elaborate patterns from the threads in the weaver's hands reflect the story of a culture, and the colors of a human soul.

With the modern world slowly creeping into Persian culture, the hand-woven and naturally dyed carpets were giving way to flawless, machine woven and artificially dyed ones. This was yet another quiet reminder of how the modern world and its great emphasis on perfectionism was, little by little, transforming the soul of this distinctive culture. In reality though, perfection isn't what gave Persian carpets their value. The unique designs and flaws within the weaves are what distinguished the carpets and gave them worth, although finding a flaw was like finding a four-leaf clover in a clover patch. It was there, somewhere, within the millions of tiny knots.

Why do some of us try so hard to be perfect? Maybe we haven't yet learned that perfection is an illusion that can

never truly be attained. Look at a four-leaf clover. The clover's perfection isn't what fascinates us so. It's the one extra petal that separates the four-leaf clover from the rest of the patch that we adore. It's the clover's imperfection that catches us off-guard and brings wonder to our eyes. It's the four-leaf clover's distinctiveness we want to press between the pages of a book and keep. It's the clover's uniqueness we appreciate.

Hopefully, we can all learn to accept our own and other's little flaws. Because, in the end, the perfection we believe we can see or can attain is only an illusion in our mind's eye. If we try to see and understand the rareness interweaved in others and things, the little imperfections, we will learn to love, cherish, and appreciate.

MUSIC

WANDERING THROUGH THE CITY, I could hear sounds of western music blare from cheap stereos in music shops on every street corner. All the music vendors played the same songs over and over again, while teenage boys crowded around, hung out, and listened at full volume to poor, bootlegged, eight-track tapes of Olivia Newton-John and the disco beats of *Saturday Night Fever* and the Bee Gees. Iranian teenagers were fascinated with western culture and hungry for any connection to the outside world.

Only a few blocks away, on the other side of Shah's Square, exotic sounds of flutes and violins from ancient Persian music softened the air. Old men working in their stalls seemed perfectly content as they listened to the music and sipped spice tea, while crafting and selling their wares.

The generation gap was too wide to ignore. Pressures from the outside world were slowly grasping hold of the future Iranian generations. The Iranian's traditional way of life was losing its balance, as western influence became more and more evident on every street corner. A few new designer boutiques, chic cafés, and discotheques in ancient mud and brick shops mixed with the old traditional vendors. The constant changes in the world around them all seemed too much, too fast, for many Iranian people to absorb. Everything old was rapidly being replaced with something new and unfamiliar, leaving no room for the familiar and old. Somehow, the picture on the streets seemed out of place, as if a culture so rich in ancient history and heritage was being thrown away and replaced with a new and different one, right before my eyes.

Walk to the other side of the street and listen to the music your ancestors played. Tradition is a ritual, a right we choose to carry from one generation to the next. Tradition helps us find meaning, purpose, and balance in our lives. If we aren't careful, though, our way of life can easily be taken away by others who don't understand, honor, or value our heritage.

Maybe we should all ponder the question, "Who has the right to throw our traditions away?" And if we relinquish them to the influences of the outside world and don't teach them to the next generation, who will be there to keep our traditions alive, to cherish them, preserve them, and give them life, so they survive through the ages?

We can hold onto the old and make room for the new, without sacrificing the values and traditions in our lives. Yes, change is a natural part of life's cycle, change makes life evolve, grow, and mature, but change doesn't mean we have to leave part of our souls behind.

When you're feeling lost, go home to what feels right. Pass your family values and traditions onto the next generation. Remember, you are the protector of your cultural way of life, in all ways, ways that can never be replaced once they're thrown away, ways your children may never have the choice to keep if they're abandoned for others beliefs.

Try to ignore pressure from the outside world and take pride in your cultural ways. This will help you feel whole. It will take you home, and give you much contentment and peace.

THE BALLOON MAN

THE ZANY BALLOON MAN HELD his head high as he roamed about Shah's Square with a bundle of balloons flapping in the breeze and a flock of children tagging behind him. The Balloon man frequently stopped to show off his skills, quickly twisting the colorful balloons into funny shapes, amusing the kids by creating popular western cartoon characters like Mickey Mouse, as if by magic. Although it wasn't the western cartoon characters that fascinated me most, it was the Balloon man's comically shaped yellow camel with a silly grin. For some reason, the funny-looking camel brought delight to my eyes, then again, caused further confusion about the world around me in my mind.

Through my eyes, the pictures on the streets were never quite clear. The confusion seemed to come from a place in the middle of two worlds in one country; the modern world and the ancient world were colliding, yet struggling to find a balance to fill the spaces inbetween.

We often lose our balance in life while our emotions struggle to find a path that feels right in our hearts. We struggle to fill the spaces inbetween, while trying to preserve certain aspects of our lives as we work through our

differences and issues with others or ourselves. At times, the confusion our struggles bring makes us feel as if we're going nowhere, but this struggle is a necessary part of our journey. This struggle is how we get from where we are to where we need to go.

Now and then, being inbetween is where we need to be. This inbetween is a place where things are working out before they can move forward into the unknown. Sometimes, being inbetween is a place we even need to stay for a while before we know what to hold onto or what to let go of. It's the place where our body discovers which path we need to take to fill the spaces inbetween two worlds—our minds and our hearts.

PERSIAN POETRY

A FEW TIMES A WEEK, NANCY DROVE me across town to Erica's house to baby sit. The morning sun lit the town as we passed by apartment buildings and small palaces with rugs draped over their terraces, and teahouses crowded with men smoking cigarettes and drinking tea.

While seeing an Iranian drinking coffee was rare, tea (*chai*) was an essential part of Iranian life. Tea was traditionally brewed in a *samovar;* a container made of copper or brass that heated the water used for making tea. Tea was always served black in a glass cup, with a side of sugar lumps, after all meals. The freshness, color, clarity, and aroma of the tea were as important as its flavor. Selling tea was also a way for many Iranian farmers to make a living, although most Iranians drank imported tea from Sri Lanka.

Teahouses were an inherent part of the Iranian community and culture. The traditional village and neighborhood teahouses were an all-male establishment—a popular place for men to hang out and discuss the latest news, while listening to readings of famous Persian poetry. This poetry was often the work of the fourteenth-century mystical poet Shams-ud-Din Muhammad, better known as Hafiz, a pen name he started to use when he began writing. Hafiz means "memorizer" and was a title given to "one who knows the Qur'an by heart."

Hafiz was the most renowned and admired of all Persian poets and, perhaps, one of the world's greatest lyricists. Nearly all Iranians, young or old, could recite small verses of Hafiz's poems. And, regardless of a family's faith, most Iranian households included his famous collection of works next to their holy book.

Hafiz's carefree writing style and thought-provoking verses expressed intense emotions of passion, romance, intimacy, love of life, God, and humanity. His poetry was often written in a light-hearted and playful manner, frequently comparing love with the intoxication of wine.

The Iranians often turned to Hafiz's words of wisdom for guidance, just as their ancestors had done for hundreds of years. In the Iranian culture, poetry was the most admired of all literary forms, probably more so there than anywhere else in the world. If a person truly wanted to know the soul of the Iranians, first becoming familiar with the timeless works of famous Persian poets, such as Hafiz, was important.

Some of us are accustomed to receiving our spiritual guidance through one person, one idea, or one conviction. We limit our spiritual growth by building our world around one source of inspiration; thus closing our hearts and minds to the wonderful gifts of wisdom that others have to share.

Maybe we should all take the time to ponder fresh ideas that stir our thoughts and emotions. Because only when we are open to new ideas can we begin to discover the true depth of our soul, and its clear connection to the world.

So keep reaching for new light in every direction you go. Because only when you reach outside your spiritual circle, to discover new points of inspiration, can you begin to understand the depth of God's light, and open your heart to the world.

The Old Brick Building

A FEW BLOCKS FROM ONE POPULAR teahouse was a tall brick building that always caught my eye. An eerie, disquieting place, it fascinated me. The sun seemed to shine on only one side as it reflected off the few tiny windows dotting the brick walls.

"What's that building?" I asked Nancy one morning when I was looking out the window.

"It's a mental institution," Nancy replied.

I didn't realize such a place existed in Isfahan. And, after that day, I often wondered how they decided it was time for someone to go to the institution because, as far as I could see, plenty of people who belonged there were still walking the city streets.

But a nightmare I had one night placed a real fear inside me. I dreamed I was lost and wondering through the streets of Isfahan passing by teahouse after teahouse, trying to find my way back home. In my dream, two Iranian policemen picked me up and took me to the mental institution simply because they couldn't understand me. No one knew I was there and I was unable to communicate with the Iranian people working in the building. When I told them I didn't belong there, they didn't know what I was saying. I felt terrified being buried in the heart of a country where I didn't understand the people and they didn't understand me. I awoke from my nightmare startled, yet relieved it was only a dream.

Although that nightmare haunted me for some time, I doubt the memory ever would have surfaced in my mind again if my life hadn't been touched by the mental illness of my older brother Mike.

At age 28, Mike was a successful business owner. He was handsome, and he had a beautiful wife and a son he adored. Mike was a loving, lighthearted person with a great sense of humor and a constant smile on his face. But the sun only shined on one side of Mike's life.

In 1985, Mike's life changed. He was diagnosed as a paranoid schizophrenic. The next ten years, he lived each day in a constant, petrifying nightmare. Mike had no relief from his dreams. He was unable to communicate his thoughts with others in a rational way. Mike's condition tore at the soul of our family. We knew how he'd been before, yet we were unable to open the door to his mind and were powerless to help him understand his pain. Somehow, I sensed his fear because I had been there before—buried in a country where I didn't understand their language and they didn't understand mine.

My nightmare ended when I woke from my dream. My brother's nightmare ended on December 15, 1994, when he died.

Sympathizing with the effects that mental illness has on a life isn't easy, unless you've been there and lived through it. You may see it every day on the streets and pass by it without understanding or even knowing. If we all could take the time to learn the signs of mental illness, we would do our families, our friends, our communities, and ourselves a great act of kindness. Then, in some small way, we may be able to make a difference in the world by helping the sun shine on both sides of someone's life.

The Four Ds

S HAWN, VANCE, AND DAMON'S PASSION for music followed them to Iran. Shawn sang, and Vance and Shawn both played lead guitar. Damon played drums. The three brothers were gifted in all forms of music. Sometimes they sat around the house harmonizing, just for fun. Listening to them entertain was refreshing. They could always lift my spirit with their great senses of humor and their music.

Shawn met Art and Dale, two American guys he worked with at Bell Helicopter. Art and Dale were also musicians. They played rhythm guitar, keyboard, and bass. Together, they all formed a rock-n-roll band, which performed at the Four Ds nightclub, located on the American base near Toufanian High School.

The Four Ds gave us a break from the perplexing world outside. This was a place to connect, let go, and have fun socializing with others from the United States, while enjoying the band's imitation sounds of famous rock-n-roll groups, such as The Carrs, Lynerd Skinyard, The Rolling Stones, Peter Frampton, and Boston.

Almost every Saturday night, I rode with the guys to the nightclub to listen to them play in front of a packed crowd of Americans and a few Iranians. Strobe lights flashed and swirled about the discotheque, while patrons drank German beer, Russian vodka, and French wine. The evenings flew by as we danced beneath the colorful lights.

I loved to sit and watch the Iranian couples dance in the midst of all the Americans. The Persian women's beautiful ethnic features were magnified with heavy make-up and red lipstick. They laced themselves in gold chains, hoop earrings, and bangle bracelets, and usually wore high-heels and form-fitting dresses, tailored in trendy European styles. A hint of expensive perfume lingered in the air around them. The men were well-groomed, with thick gold chains around their necks. Most wore John Travolta-style polyester jackets and flair pants.

But what fascinated me most was how effortlessly the couples found their rhythm in the band's rock-n-roll music. They danced on the hard floor in an exotic Egyptian style, whirling, twisting, turning, and swaying in smooth flowing motions. The women's bangle bracelets seemed to keep rhythm to the music, like tambourines jangling, as their arms sashayed to the beat. As they danced, the couples seemed able to adapt and find their own cultural rhythm in any music they listened to.

My passion for dancing was as strong as the guys' passion for music. I loved to dance the night away because it gave me the freedom to let go. It was as if stepping back to what I was familiar with helped me adapt and move forward into the unfamiliar world outside. The Four Ds was a place that, for only a few hours a week, took me back home.

Music is a powerful force. It takes us away—not only our bodies, but our spirits too. Music moves and heals our souls. It helps bring balance, perspective, and validation to our thoughts and feelings where, sometimes, there seems

to be none. Music provides the rhythm we need to adapt and dance to life's magic.

We naturally take the step that feels right, the step that makes us feel most free. We waltz slowly, with grace, passion, class, and dignity. We tango quickly, with intensity, vigor, zest, and fun. We tap lightly, with charm, enchantment, and humor. The dance is all in how we hear the music around us and how we choose to move to its beat.

But the dance, just as life, can be filled with many twists and turns. We may go through a lot of stumbling to get where we need to go. We may even have to step back and try the dance all over again before we can gracefully move forward into the unknown.

Listen to the music around you. Really listen. What do you hear? How do you feel? What are you listening and dancing to? Does the music you hear move your soul? Does the music touch your heart? Does it render your spirit to dance? Does it take you back home? If not, find what soothes and invigorates you. Find inspiration in all you hear and dance to.

The Rooftop

Vance sometimes joined me on our flat rooftop where I read and soaked up the sun in the parching 100-degree-plus summertime heat. We could hear commotion coming from the *koche* below, but no one could see or hear us. The rooftops were private, off limits, not the proper place to be, unless, of course, there was an emergency, so we felt safe and we could relax, knowing no one would find us up there sunbathing.

One afternoon while Vance and I were lying in the sun, we heard a loud noise from the backyard of our neighbor's house. Curious, we tiptoed to the rooftop edge and peeked down inside his yard. We could hardly believe what we saw. The view was nothing like we expected. We found ourselves gazing into another world—an ancient world.

Our neighbor's courtyard was filled with primitive pieces—some junk, some simply old—like huge vases filled with water, old pottery dusted with fresh flour, and broken clay bowls, pots and cups scattered about the ground. Worn-out Persian carpets were draped over the balcony, ancient stained-glass windows covered the backside of the house, and a primitive stone pit used for cooking still smoldered. In the midst of all this, beautiful yellow roses were in full bloom around a traditional Persian fountain in the center of the courtyard.

Our neighbors had lived there all along, but we hadn't taken the time to get to know them. Only when we peeked into their private world did we begin to understand their timeless way of life.

Feeling a little guilty about invading our neighbors' privacy, we retreated to our bedroom. We sat on the foot of our bed, gazing out the window, still in awe at what we saw framed inside the neighbors' walls. Then, out of nowhere, we heard rapid footsteps and then we saw two uniformed Iranian policemen jumping over the rooftops and running toward our house. One policeman was shouting— "*bali, bali*" (yes, yes) indicating to the other policeman to follow him. We froze—frightened they were coming to get us for peeking into our neighbors' courtyard. Vance and I fell to the bedroom floor, lying there trembling. We were terrified because we didn't know the punishment for invading the privacy of others' homes, but we knew what we'd done was taboo in Iran.

The policemen stopped next to our bedroom window, their conversation and tone-of-voice serious. We held our breath, lying still, afraid to look out the window for fear they might see us move or hear us breathe. Finally, the men's voices grew faint. Only then did Vance muster-up enough courage to check outside. After he reassured me all was okay, I looked to see for myself. We watched as the men continued to move over rooftop after rooftop until finally they disappeared out of sight.

I knew we would never know for certain why the policemen came our way, but after that day, I never again looked over the rooftop into the privacy of our neighbors' world.

*At times, we may try to glimpse in to the privacy of oth-
ers' worlds. We may do this innocently, from a natural*

curiosity, to understand our brother or sister's way of life. We may believe we're doing no harm by overstepping our boundaries. But no matter how innocent our actions may be, we really have no right to invade the privacy of others. We have no right to be present in our neighbors' life unless we're invited. If others want us in their world, they'll open the door to their hearts and ask us graciously, welcoming us into their homes through increased trust, respect, and acceptance.

THE BRITS

OUR FAMILY WAS OCCASIONALLY invited to pool parties and barbecues at the British compound, located out across the desert, in the middle of nowhere. The modern, box-shaped houses at the compound all looked alike. The center of the grounds had a large park-like setting with barbecues and a gigantic swimming pool. But it wasn't the houses, barbecues, or swimming I enjoyed the most about being at the British compound. It was our British friends wonderful sense of humor. They took life so lightly, seeming not to have a care in the world. They lived each moment of every day, finding humor in everything. My stomach would ache from laughing so much at the Brits' outlook on life and their silly, off-the-wall sense of humor. Their lively spirit was so fun-loving, and instantly contagious.

Most of the time a little laughter softens the harshness and lightens the seriousness of our souls. Humor sees sunlight in the rain and, in the darkness, it lets the light shine through again. For a moment, a little humor can take away our cares and worries.

Make laughter contagious. Make it a part of your daily life because, if you look for it, humor really is out there—

everywhere. You only need to change your perspective, open your eyes, and lighten your heart. Then you'll see and feel humor all around you—everywhere—even out in the middle of nowhere.

THE EYE OF MY SOUL

CONTRARY TO THE DARK, MOONLIT city I saw on the first night of our arrival, the daylight sun warmed and penetrated the desert sand, casting a shimmering mirage over the whole city. As I strolled by palaces and mosques, I could see the Iranians' testimony of pride, their spirit of patriotism, and their determination to survive displayed in the architecture and culture surrounding me. Through my eyes, there was no question as to the nation's significant place in ancient history. As my understanding of the Iranians grew, my heart gradually softened toward their way of life and their deep religious beliefs. That's why I found several stories Ed told us so disquieting.

One story was about a drunk American man who shot an Iranian cab driver in the head over a taxi fare and the other was about American teenage boys who rode motorbikes through the city's treasured blue-tiled Royal Mosque. But the story I found most disturbing was of three American women who, several years before our arrival, strolled through Shah's Square one Friday, and then deliberately wandered into the Friday Mosque dressed in skimpy clothes, intentionally giggling and talking loudly with a total disregard for the Muslim people's place of worship and day of holy prayer.

Ed told us one story after another of Americans offending the Iranian people on their own soil. But those U.S. citizens who crossed the people's boundaries or broke the law received no fines or trials. This was because, as American citizens, the Shah gave them immunity under an agreement with the United States, an agreement that seemed to give a few Americans permission to totally disregard the country's cultural ways.

These stories were all in contrast to the simple signs of respect and admiration we received from the Iranian people. Such as teenage girls peeking from beneath their veils, giggling and glancing back at us when we passed them. And the women who were captivated by the symbol of purity that Vance and Damon's white hair represented that politely asked in Farsi, "Could I touch?" fascinated as they ran their fingers though the fine strands of pale hair. Even the glares from the elderly women showed some tolerance and respect toward us. Only devotion to their faith created their disapproving eyes of the way we dressed.

But Ed's stories, the giggling girls, the women, and even the elderly women weren't what helped me realize how out of place we must have been. Instead, it was the children's natural curiosity as they stopped to gawk at us, their big brown eyes taking in our strange appearance and western clothing, as we casually strolled through the streets in T-shirts, sneakers, and faded bell-bottom blue jeans.

I had to respect the Iranian people's social manners. They were a gracious, kind, and happy people. They just weren't sure what to think of the Americans who had inundated their country with cultural ideas of materialism and technology from the west.

A prickly thorn seemed to poke at my conscience. I felt somehow we'd stepped into a sacred part of the Iranian people's world with no respect for their cultural ways. It was as if we were somehow accountable for contaminating Persian soil with materialism from the western world. We seemed to have crossed the boundaries of the Persian people with little appreciation for their ancient civilization, or recognition of its historical place in the world.

Maybe we should all ask ourselves, "Have I crossed over my boundaries into someone's life, without respect to their differences? Have I tried to force my ways on them without respect to their inner identity?"

Maybe it's time we all learn to truly appreciate others' differences. Understanding that in order for peace and harmony to take place in our world we must accept others' ways. When we understand the power of this kind of acceptance and work it into our daily graces, our lives will change. When we learn to expect that others will respond, believe, and see differently from us, our compassion, love, and acceptance for them will flourish. The moment we see it any other way, the possibility of peace and harmony diminishes. So try to respect the reality that we are all human beings, the same, yet distinct, in our own ways. Respect others' differences by valuing the diversity in life.

PART SEVEN

SUMMER VACATION

The World Is a Theatre of Love.

—An Indian (Kashmiri) proverb

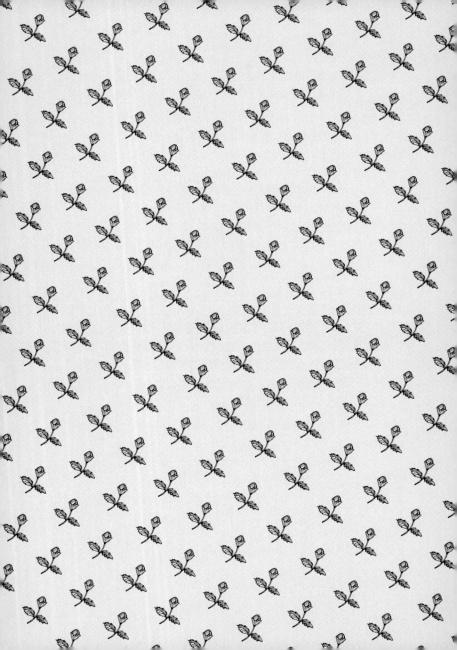

THE DRIVE TO TEHRAN

W E WERE FINALLY OFF ON OUR long-awaited family summer vacation to Thailand. The long, bumpy, 200-mile drive across the sweltering hot desert to Tehran that first week in August was exciting but, also miserable. Ed, Nancy, Heather, Vance, and I were all crammed into a small rental car with no air conditioner. Shawn, Damon, and Kurt followed behind us in a roomy rented truck. Ed opted for us to drive to Tehran rather than fly. He said the money we saved in airfare would give us more money to spend on our vacation in Thailand.

We arrived in Tehran around midnight, cranky from the hot, crowded, miserable drive through the desert. We only wanted to stretch our legs before checking into the hotel, where we expected to grab a few hours' sleep before catching our predawn flight to Thailand. Our plans quickly changed, though, after Ed spent some time wheeling and dealing with the hotel manager on the price of our rooms. The manager, believing we were wealthy Americans, wouldn't budge from his price. And Ed refused to pay the ridiculously high price the manager had quoted. Of course we all agreed with Ed that the room prices were much too high for us to get only a few hours' sleep.

So there we were, all eight of us, in the lavishly decorated hotel lobby well after midnight with no place to go until our morning flight. With a stack of luggage piled at our sides, legs and arms swung over plush white lobby furniture, we all fell asleep on the couch, chairs, and carpets that covered the hotel's marble floors. No one seemed to care if we were sleeping there, not even the manager who, so stubbornly, had stuck to his price.

At times, we may go to silly lengths to prove a point. Sometimes it's to make a few dollars and sometimes it's to save a few, but sometimes the point we're trying to prove has nothing to do with the issue. It only has to do with our unwillingness to compromise.

If we aren't careful, though, our stubbornness can take control of our lives. We may say, "This is the way it's going to be and nothing you can do or say will change my mind." By saying this, we leave no room for compromise or common ground. We close our eyes because we've already made up our minds, no matter what the final cost.

We don't always need to agree with others and we don't always need to see eye to eye. Sometimes it's appropriate to be stubborn and resist others' ways. But if we make this way of connecting with others a normal part of our business and daily lives, then, in the end, who really pays the price?

DISCOVERING THAILAND

B EFORE I KNEW IT, WE WERE standing with our heaps of luggage in the midst of a busy sidewalk in front of our hotel in downtown Bangkok. As far as we could see up and down the street was a never-ending obstacle of noisy traffic, snarled up with small cars, taxis, public trolleys, and buses. No wonder so many Thai people rode mopeds and bicycles or simply walked.

After settling in to our hotel room, Nancy, Heather, and I took a colorful, strange-looking, three-wheeled taxi called a *tuktuk* to Siam Square, where we shopped in a maze of floors in the largest mall I'd ever seen. Mannequins posed in the display windows were dressed in fashions I'd expect to see in the boutiques of downtown Manhattan or Paris, not in Bangkok. The mannequins modeled fashionable, straight-legged pants and I still wore bell-bottom jeans. The shop's trendy clothes were meticulously stitched and the prices were cheap, a fraction of what they would have cost in Iran or the United States.

At Martin's Custom Tailor, just down the road from our hotel, we all had clothes tailor-made from the shop's endless selection of fabrics and patterns. An autographed picture of a young Bob Hope hung on the wall behind the cash register and the owner insisted Mr. Hope was a regular customer, who often had silk suits tailor-made there. I had no doubt that Mr. Hope frequented the shop, after I saw how effortlessly the little Thai seamstresses fashioned top-quality pieces. My favorite tailor-made clothes were an up-to-date pair of straight-leg jeans and an elegant iridescent, peach-colored silk dress.

We had an exciting fun-filled weekend on Pattaya Beach. There we sipped on fresh Mai Tais while relaxing, near our hotel, under the palm trees. We rode water scooters in the warm, crystal blue sea. And explored the sandy white beach, where we spent hours hunting for puka shells along the shoreline. One afternoon, we even caught sight of a gigantic, shiny, black tropical snake slithering into a small cave. We lost all track of time under the sun, waiting for the snake to reappear, and by evening we were all bright red.

Nevertheless, our fun in Thailand continued the next day when we arrived at the Crocodile Farms—not far from Bangkok. There we visited a petting zoo, rode on amusement park rides, and watched bold Thai men wrestle alligators in the swamps. We capped off the day by sitting around the park perimeter, where we relaxed and enjoyed the Thai spirit festival performed by colorful masked dancers.

The following day we took a ferry through Damnoen Saduak floating market, where a variety of merchandise and food was sold off boats floating in the murky canal. The floating market was a city of its own, where some Thai people carried on their daily lives in boats and ramshackle huts bordering the river.

We visited lavish, golden Buddhist Temples where we watched ancient temple prints being reproduced on rice paper. The majority of Thai people were practicing Buddhists and Buddhist monks—young and old were an inherent part of Bangkok's landscape. We could easily spot their shiny baldheads and bright orange robes at a distance. Thailand's happy, harmonious way of life and emphasis on the sacredness of family and friends was mainly because of Buddhism's traditional value systems inborn into the Thai society.

The Suan Sam Phram Rose Gardens were about twenty miles from Bangkok. These gardens were filled with fragrant roses of every variety, size, and color imaginable. The roses bloomed next to sweet, lush orchards that thrived in gushing streams, which rose and fell through tropical green foliage. The rose gardens were all I ever imagined paradise to be with tropical birds, and monkeys dancing and singing, as if they were on stage performing the perfect finale. We even watched show elephants moving teak-wood logs as they traditionally did in the forests. After a short break, the elephants were available for tourists to ride for a small fee. Vance and I crawled on a gigantic elephant's back. We were intimidated by the animal's size, but unable to stop smiling as it carried us around the grounds, swaying us from side to side, while slowly lifting its huge legs.

We even had fun running for cover from the downpour of the monsoon rains. The rains dumped sheets of warm water on the ground, flooding the creeks that ran through the gardens. We quickly learned the painted paper umbrellas we purchased a few hours earlier weren't umbrellas at all—they were parasols, and their fragile structure was no match for the torrential storm. In a matter of seconds, the showers completely drenched us. We found shelter under the eaves of a quaint little restaurant, where we ate hot, spicy noodle soup and strange-looking fruit, while watching a double rainbow fade away as the sun returned again.

Add fun and adventure to your life. Explore all you can. Who says you have to limit your fun to a particular event, day, or vacation? The world is full of fun and you don't have to go to a tropical island to find it. Let go of your umbrella. Throw your hands to the sky. Run in the rain and feel the raindrops soak your face. Instead of waiting for fun to happen, make fun a part of your life each and every day.

THE UNREST BEGINS

W HILE WE WERE ENJOYING our vacation in Bangkok, we
began to hear of unrest on the streets in Iran. By mid
August, the front pages of the Thai newspapers headlined the
tragic death of over four hundred Iranian people, mostly women
and children, who were trapped in a Tehran theater and then
burned alive while watching a popular Iranian film. Iranian people took to the streets, rioting when rumors spread that the theater doors had intentionally been locked by the Shah's secret
police, *Savak*. Coincidently, these rumors created fertile ground
for the exiled Ayatollah Khomeini's Islamic regime to surface
again. Thousands upon thousands of Iranian people who had
stayed neutral in the struggle that had been building for years
between the Shah and Islamic extremist Ayatollah Khomeini
unexpectedly shifted to the side of Khomeini's regime. The horrifying event at the theater created a state of unrest in Iran and
uncertainty in the minds of Muslim and non-Muslim people as
to which political side they should proclaim they were on.

We had left Isfahan over a week earlier and we found it hard
to believe the world news we were hearing pertained to Iran. Even
more worrisome, though, was how the turmoil could manifest so
quickly because we hadn't seen any outward signs of instability
before we left the country. Ed and Nancy didn't seem too worried
about the uprising because they'd witnessed small protests in Iran

before. They reassured us life would be back to normal by the time we returned home. Knowing the situation was completely out of their hands, they believed the best thing for us to do was not to worry and continue with our vacation as planned.

We often worry about what will happen next. But really, what good does it do to worry about a situation over which we have no control? Worrying can't stop or change the event. Worrying only makes us become more anxious or stressed.

Try not to worry about events that are out of your hands because, in reality, worrying won't change a thing. Maybe the healthy thing to do is to continue on the best way we can with the life we had planned, finding comfort in the thought that life will change. Things won't stay the same forever and we can't control some things in life, no matter how much we worry.

PHUKET BEACH

W E PACKED AND THEN HEADED out on a long, commercial bus ride through Thailand's countryside, watching lush, tropical scenery flash by us. Along the way, we passed village people carrying baskets of food while they moved herds of thin cows down mountain roads.

In the distance, we watched oxen pulling plows, and native Thai men and women in wide-brimmed straw hats working from dawn until dusk, knee-deep in miles and miles of wet rice fields. Rice was one of the main sources of revenue in Thailand. The rice plantations, which had fed Thai people for centuries, were intricately trenched and irrigated. Ed said that in late spring, near the end of the dry season, the fields were alive with farmers turning the soil. A month or so later, after the rains came, water covered the patties growing with young rice sprouts. Harvest time was in the autumn, when the rains had passed and the grain turned yellow. Extravagant festivals followed the harvest and the burning of the reaped fields. Then the soil was prepared, once again, for another cycle of cultivation.

Our final destination was a little-known vacation spot, at the time, called Phuket Beach. The thriving landscape was so natural and untainted compared to the commercial streets and beaches of Bangkok. The seemingly effortless way of life and picturesque setting was like a breath of fresh air. Few tourists could be seen around town or on the beaches.

Phuket Beach had a tranquility in which we could truly relax and enjoy the beautiful paradise surrounding us. We slept in small fisherman bungalows built along the beach. Mosquito nets were draped over our beds at night and natural, lukewarm water was available for showers in the morning. And, only thin shafts of light from the sun or moon filtering through the shutters, lit up the inside of the bungalows.

A quaint little food stand, made of bamboo shoots and a palm-leaf roof, built on the beach in the open air, served as our daily restaurant. Nutritious fresh fish—the catch of the day—was available for each meal. The restaurant owner and his children picked fresh pineapples every morning from a grove behind the hut. The refreshing pineapples, cut into fancy shapes then placed in a jar on a beach picnic table, quickly became my favorite snack.

One serene morning, as the sun rose over the water and the silhouettes of the palm trees had nearly faded away, we all stepped from the beach into a small boat owned by the fisherman who operated the food stand. The fisherman and his son ferried us across the bay to a small island flourishing with tropical vegetation. There, we drank sweet milk from coconuts we picked off the trees, while unruly monkeys, swinging from tree to tree, shrieked and squealed at us, as if protesting our presence.

We quickly blended into the natural scenery surrounding us on Phuket Beach. By day, we lived in our swimsuits with the hot sun kissing our skin and warm, white sand sifting through our toes. By night, we fell asleep to the calming rhythm of waves caressing the shoreline. Life was so simple, pure, and refreshing there that we had no need for the modern world and, each day, it became more and more apparent how nourishing the surroundings were to our well-being.

Late one afternoon, Vance and I were lying on the beach enjoying the sensation of warm water rippling against our feet when I noticed how amazingly peaceful my mind and body were. That day, for the first time in my life, I felt the sweet touch of serenity move through me. I thought—all Vance and I will ever need is right here on Phuket Beach.

I learned a special lesson while vacationing on Phuket Beach. I learned how serene life can be if it isn't filled with all the clutter and distractions that come from the material world. The natural warmth and way of life on Phuket beach was so simple. Nature carried on there feeding us with exactly what we needed to nurture our bodies, minds, and spirits. The vegetation, the sea, the sun, the moon, and the fresh air all combined gave us life, a pure and simple life, as pure and simple as life can be.

Some of us have come to believe that the necessities of life are the material goods we possess. But all we really need was right there on Phuket Beach.

So do your mind-set a favor and sell a thing or two, then take a trip to Phuket Beach, if not in body, in spirit. Then come back refreshed with what you truly need— serenity of the soul, minus all the clutter.

The Show

AFTER A WEEK OF VACATIONING on Phuket Beach, the time had come to return to reality—the hustle and bustle of downtown Bangkok. There, we enjoyed our last few days in Thailand, strolling through shops in the daytime and living it up after dusk.

Bangkok's nightlife brought with it a whole new crowd. As we walked through dark ramshackle districts toward Pat pong Street, each step of the way got brighter. In the heart of the city, while the men and women who worked in the floating markets and rice fields slept, the prostitutes, pimps, and other disreputable people began to work under flashy neon lights. The lights lit up brothels, hotels, nightclubs, massage parlors, and bars.

Entering the center of the notorious Pat pong district, we saw the lifestyle change before our eyes. The flashy neon lights and sinful mood of Pat pong Street couldn't have been a more glaring contrast to the serene beaches and golden Buddhist temples that gave Thailand its virtue.

Brothels, whorehouses, go-go bars, and pubs were jammed with patrons and whores. Errand boys, who worked for the underground nightclubs, approached us with big smiles as we walked down the sidewalks, asking bluntly in broken English, "You like see live sex show?" Prostitutes—barely dressed in provocative short shorts and halter-tops—tried to lure men into the brothels. "You like have sex with me?" the girls asked, reassuring the men with their innocent smiles and flirtatious eyes that they could arrange anything. But Ed responded by politely shaking his head "no" as we moved onward, passing brothel after brothel.

One messenger boy caught our attention when he asked, "You like see live banana show?" Then, raising his eyebrows he said, "Just two bucks." Ed gave in to the boy's charm and agreed to take us all to the show (with the exception of Heather, who was being cared for back at the hotel). Ed thought the show might be something we all needed to see—a sad part of the culture but, nevertheless, a reality of life in Thailand.

I was reluctant to go, yet curious all the same, so I tagged along anyway. The boy disappeared after introducing us to a small Thai man who led us through a dark, quiet alley, reassuring us all the way that we would be "very, very happy and pleased with show." Opening a door, he led us down a short flight of stairs where we heard western rock music blaring from behind another door that lead into a large showroom. Somewhat embarrassed, I lowered my head, hiding behind Vance as we made our way through the crowded, smoke-filled underground bar. We all sat at a round table in front of the stage.

The show was already in progress, with a small, nicely built Thai man and his beautiful young wife at center stage. The nude dancers moved with elegance on the stage. The man used a banana on his partner, stirring her physical being as she accepted his moves gracefully. Dropping the banana toward the end of the act, they connected and then continued elegantly dancing in harmony as if one being.

The gracefulness of the choreography surprised me; it wasn't at all what I'd expected. It wasn't dirty and nasty like I thought it would be. The bond between the two dancers was equal, with both enjoying an artistic connection that could only come from a true of trust and love. Yet, I knew the reality of it all. They were performing an act to make a living. They were exploiting their bodies to survive.

The couple bowed out. Their show was over and after a short pause the next show began.

We each have the right to enjoy our sexual nature, and take pleasure in the gift of being human. But we must remember to enjoy this gift without exploiting others or ourselves. We can do this by simply cherishing our companion's love and respecting their boundaries, in public and in private.

We will always know when our companion's touch is the gift of love, because our body, mind, heart, and soul tell us this, the moment we feel the security of trust that comes with the fulfillment of love. This trust allows two spirits and two bodies to dance as one, through the rhythm of a pure and simple bond of true love. But only two hearts, alone, behind closed doors can truly treasure this beautiful gift of being human, and in love.

THE CHUBBY ONE

A CHUBBY THAI GIRL APPEARED from the corner of the stage. She couldn't have been much older than thirteen. She was dressed in short-shorts, with no top covering her young breasts. As the music began to play, she shyly moved forward to center stage. She hung her head low as she stared at the floor under her feet. Her trembling body tried desperately to keep rhythm to the music. She tapped her feet fast when she should have tapped them slow and slow when she should have tapped them fast. Tears of innocence filled her eyes as her limp arms and legs moved out of beat. Despite her inexperience, she kept moving her body, trying to connect with the music's rhythm.

The young girl was obviously scared. My heart sank. I wanted to run up and hold her. I wanted to tell her she didn't have to continue. I wanted to shake her and tell her she didn't have to expose her body for money. I wanted to tell her all the money in the world didn't matter if it wasn't earned with a clear conscience. And if I'd had a little more nerve, I might have done just that.

As the girl's performance was about to end, the doors to the room flew open and a mob of policemen entered to close the place down. All the patrons, including our group, quickly grabbed their belongings and fled out a side door, narrowly avoiding being arrested.

I was glad I didn't have to witness the innocence of another dancer's life being taken away. I don't know if I could have watched another girl go through what I saw this young girl do. She obviously didn't belong there but, for whatever reason, she was there, with shame and humiliation written across her face. And as the thought crossed my mind, I realized if she continued dancing each night, her confidence would build. She would block out her conscience, while carving a niche for her livelihood by exploiting herself.

The exploitation of sex is seen when we force our bodies to move against our conscience, when we attach our sexual beings with anything other than a pure heart.

If we exploit ourselves, the encounter may weigh heavy on our consciences, where it lingers and follows us wherever we go. The shame and humiliation we feel may be revealed in all we do and say. It may appear in how we interact with others, and how we look at the world around us. Our conscience is meant to be kept pure and clean. Our body is the dwelling place for our conscience so, ultimately, what we do to our body touches our spirit too.

Occasionally we may go against our morals, not realizing the effect this could have on our spirit until later. If this happens, hopefully we will learn from the experience and can somehow find a way to be at peace with ourselves. But we should always strive to live our life with a clear conscience and avoid events that might create regret in our lives. And one way to do this is to always remember that only the bond of love we feel when we dance in rhythm with our partner truly fulfills our sexual being. Only sex with love can give us a clear conscience.

GROUNDED

THE LAST DAY OF OUR VACATION in Thailand, we took a guided boat to Coral Island. There we snorkeled in shallow waters, viewing the bright tropical fish and the neon-colored coral reefs that thrived under the sea.

After spending three weeks in Thailand, discovering a culture so colorful, warm, and full of life, we could hardly believe that our adventures in the country were coming to an end. The Thai people had been so respectful toward our family, making us feel very welcome in their country. The people's cheerful manner and their relentless chatter had been uplifting and even though we didn't understand many words of their language, they didn't seem to mind. They still smiled and giggled at us, no matter what we understood or said.

Now we had to pack and catch our flight to India for our last week of summer vacation. Ed said he liked to stop in India each year after his vacation in Thailand. He explained that, somehow, India grounded him, by reminding him of the other realities of life and that, after visiting India, Iran seemed like paradise, making the transition from Thailand back home to Isfahan a much easier adjustment.

We can fly high in the sky with our feet off the ground, where everything is beautiful, fun, and enchanting, where the true realities of life are at a distance. But we can't stay up there forever. We have to come down sometime. Down to Earth, where we live. This is where reality steps in and gently taps us on the shoulders, saying this is the way life is. And this is usually when we need to see reality the most.

Reality is in the moment—where we're standing right now. Reality is what we see before our eyes. Reality is where we always need to return, to absorb where we've been. Reality is where we need to be to learn and grow. Reality takes us home.

NEW DELHI

W HEN WE STEPPED OFF THE PLANE at the airport near New Delhi, I began to understand what Ed meant, as the hot, humid air fell on us like raindrops from the sultry sky.

The streets of downtown New Delhi were filled with barefoot, pot-bellied children of all ages. These children tugged at our clothes with filthy hands, while looking up at us with their sun-baked faces and precious, big brown eyes begging for coins, so they could buy something to eat. The mothers held their limp babies out toward us, desperately pleading for help through the hollow look in their eyes. Ed told us that some of the babies had intentionally been drugged, so they appeared sick, and the mother's plea for help was often a dramatic act, performed on a daily basis, to make a living.

The crippled and the amputees, lucky enough to have a means of transportation, commuted around town on handcrafted four-wheeled scooters, which they moved through the streets by pushing their hands back and forth on the polluted ground. Ed said, at one time the Indian government tried to clean up the streets by building shelters for the homeless people. The shelters were suppose to be a safe haven from the elements outside where the beggars could have their basic needs meet. But the beggars gradually returned to the streets where the living was more lucrative and they felt much more at home. Most government shelters were eventually shut down.

Sidewalks were packed with peddlers selling herbs, spices, and colorful merchandise, such as handcrafted tapestries and leatherworks, embroidered and mirrored silk and wool garments, and brass pots and pans, vases, and incense burners. The goods hung from racks or were neatly spread on blankets or tables. Craftsmen who squatted illegally on the sidewalks hoped to sell their goods before a policeman came along waving a baton to make them scurry away. If a squatter happened to see an officer coming their way, they would quickly bundle up their merchandise by gathering all four sides of their blanket, and then quickly move down the sidewalk to the next street corner.

Affluent Indian businessmen seemed out of place in the poverty in the streets. They were typically dressed in silk suits and ties, with polished gold rings decorating their fingers. The men stood tall, proud, and dignified with crisp, clean turbans, wrapped and piled high on their heads. To my surprise, some even had stunning blue-green eyes that sparkled against their olive skin. The businessmen's appearance was an obvious contrast to the beady-eyed, tiny men dressed in soiled rag clothes who were begging on the streets.

Indian women traditionally wore elegant saris, loosely wrapped around them. Saris were similar to chadors, only made of silk in colorful hues of bright yellow, blue, greens, and reds. Wealthy women adorned themselves with gold jewelry and precious stones, which were draped around their arms and necks, and pierced their ears and noses. The dot on the center of many Indian women's foreheads was not only a decorative mark and an indication of marital status but, also, a reminder for them to focus their lives on God. But surrounding them, as well as us and others on the streets, was a disquieting, endless poverty that seemed accepted as a normal way of life, it was as if we were all blind to the depth of God's image right before their eyes.

How easy it is for the wealthy to separate themselves from the poor. I saw this division on the streets of India among Hindu, in Iran among Muslim, in Thailand among Buddhist, and, each day, I see it in America among Christians. This separation has no borders.

How easy it is to pass by God's image on the street and not even see Him. Yes, God is beautiful, God is love, but God can be unpleasant too, as He teaches us about the consequence of self-righteousness. Maybe He intentionally makes life this way because, for others to see God in us, we must first see God in them. No matter how destitute, sick, or repulsive others may be, we should love them as God does, unconditionally.

But we don't always want to see the unpleasant side of God. It's disquieting to our souls, so we ignore it, closing our eyes to the reality it brings. We block out the poverty from our minds by turning the other way, justifying our actions by saying the poor must have managed their lives badly for their lives to turn out that way. But, maybe, we turn the other way because the poverty is a quiet reminder of where we could be if our lives had turned out differently.

To many of us, our belief in God is an essential part of our lives. We use special symbols or objects to focus on Him. We set aside special places and special times to worship Him. We need to remember, though, that all we really need to do is quiet ourselves, look around, then focus our hearts and eyes on what we see before us—each moment of every day. Only then will we see God alive, right where He has always been and will always be. We will sense the presence of His love living in each person we meet, and in everything we see.

THE GIRL BY THE BRICK WALL

MY STOMACH TURNED WHEN I smelled the musty, humid air, mixed with the odor of urine coming from public commodes as we strolled down the streets in New Delhi. The smell intensified as we rounded a busy city street corner. I noticed a young woman, who couldn't have been much older than me. She was lying on the ground in the shade behind a brick wall that was covered with mildew near a restroom. She was dressed in heavy layers of soiled, shredded garments, her eyes loosely closed, and no shoes on her swollen, blue feet.

As we approached, I noticed flies swarming around her, landing on her face, and in the corners of her eyes and mouth. I waited for her to lift her hand to swat them away, but she didn't. I watched for a sign of life—the blink of an eye, the twitch of a hand, her breath moving her body, but there was none. It was as if her soul had left her, leaving behind only the hollow shell of her body on the ground.

Ed nudged me to move down the sidewalk and ignore her. I could only watch the young women grow smaller and smaller, until, finally, she disappeared out of sight. Ed reassured me that the police would eventually find her lying there and have her body carried away, but his words gave me no peace of mind, knowing that the girl had lost her life without comfort as people passed her, blind to her needs. She was too young for her life to have ended that way. She was too young to have died without dignity on the street.

Nothing is more powerful than the finality of death. It brings us back to reality. It moves us to search our souls and reflect on the true priorities of life. Death reminds us of the inevitable. It reminds us that someday we, too, will be gone. The realism of death brings us back to our centers, moving us to share the love in our hearts with others living in our lives today. We begin to understand the power of love and how it needs to be integrated into everyone's life. Love that insures the dignity and comfort of death, no matter who the person is or where they are.

The act of loving and caring for one another must come to us as effortlessly as living and breathing hour after hour, day after day and year after year until we die. Each of us leaving behind our legacy of love to be passed down from generation to generation, so love never disappears, so love is never passed by—so love never dies.

THE TAJ MAHAL

ACCORDING TO THE WORLD NEWS and the photographs in Indian newspapers, the unrest in Iran was escalating. Sporadic riots and looting were being reported in Tehran and other major cities in the country. Ed decided we should cut short our vacation in India, which meant we wouldn't be able to visit the Taj Mahal as planned.

The Taj Mahal, a white marble mausoleum built in the mid 1600s by Shah Jehan in memory of his favorite wife, Mumtaz Mahal, is located in Agra, a few hours south of Delhi. The Taj Mahal is a blend of Muslim and Hindu architectural styles. Building this massive structure, which has a central dome and minarets on each corner, took some 20,000 workers. Each facade was inlaid with semiprecious stones.

The Taj Mahal is a reflection of India to the world and an inspiring example of how beautiful the world can be when different cultures work side by side in harmony to celebrate love for others.

Even though we were all disappointed we couldn't visit the Taj Mahal, we knew the time had come to return home. Each day, Ed appeared more and more anxious about the unrest in Iran. He needed to return home to see for himself what was happening in the country. We packed and flew back home to Isfahan, with only a postcard of the Taj Mahal as a memento.

Others often try to tell us what's happening in the world around us or what the outcome to a particular situation in our life may be. We may naively close our eyes to their words—we don't take them seriously. Even though they may speak the truth, we continue to believe and see only what we want to believe and see.

Sometimes for us to believe the words of others, we must first see the situation for ourselves, in our own minds and through our own hearts. Sometimes all the pictures and words in the world don't have any influence on us if we can't see and believe the truth for ourselves. But isn't this what life's lessons are all about? Truths that come and go and change our outlook on the realities of life, truths we can only learn through our own minds, eyes, hearts, and souls. Truths we must see to believe.

PART EIGHT

A TURN OF EVENTS

Hope is born of Despair.

—An Iranian proverb

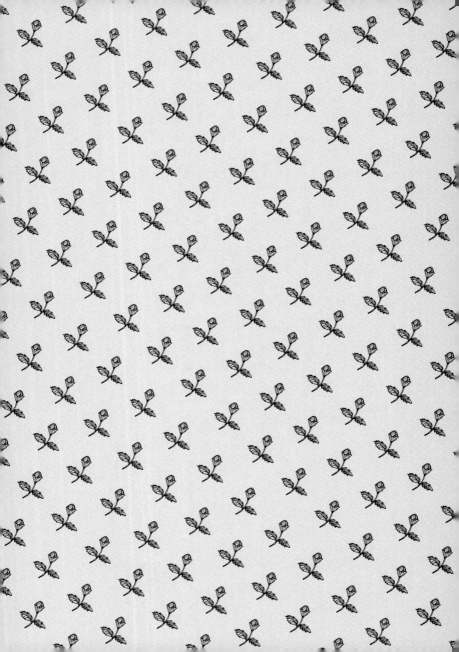

Back Home in Isfahan

ETURNING TO ISFAHAN FROM vacation in late August, we witnessed something out of the ordinary, disquieting, and off-balance from when we had left. While we were away, Americans had been advised by the U.S. Embassy to keep a low profile inside Iran's borders. Iranian soldiers heavily patrolled the cities. Isfahan had lost its zest and zeal. And the normal rhythm of the daily hustle and bustle of life on the streets had disappeared.

Iranian people reacted different toward us. We sensed whispers in the air as we made our way through the eerily quiet streets, trying to carry on our daily lives as if we didn't notice the difference. Every move we made seemed to be watched by the ordinary people and the merchants who stood at the front doors of their shops. A few shopkeepers kindly warned us to be aware of what was happening around us, while politely letting us know they had to disassociate themselves from us for the safety of their families and businesses. This wasn't what they wanted, they said, but they did it from fear of what the Islamic extremists might do to them if they continued befriending us. Most shopkeepers distanced themselves from us altogether, no longer haggling us to step into their shops, and the bazaar merchants' good-natured spirits disappeared.

Music shops were deserted and silent. Other merchants drew their metal gates down halfway, closing early some days and, on other days, not opening at all from the fear of rumored demonstrations and riots by Islamic extremists.

Under growing pressure from conservative Muslim sects, such as the *Hezbollah*, many Iranian women, who, long ago, had abandoned their veils, believed covering their heads with chadors or scarves when leaving their home was best for their safety. And, out of fear, many of these women quit wearing face make up. With their children clinging tightly to their sides, the women kept to themselves, quickly gathering their daily supplies from local vendors. Then, hanging their heads low and without pausing to visit others along the way, the women hurried back home where they felt safe.

The men's prayer rituals became much more intense. Oblivious to the world around them, they held on tightly to their worry beads (prayer beads), counting each stone over and over, while meditating and praying as they walked down the streets.

The picture of Iran's future turned bleak early in September when the Shah imposed martial law throughout Iran, after demonstrations in Tehran—at the end of the Ramadan holy period—called for the return of Khomeini. The following Friday, thousands upon thousands of Iranians marched down a busy thoroughfare in the country's capital. The marchers headed toward a squad of armed soldiers who had been ordered to halt any demonstrations against the Shah. Without warning, the soldiers pumped round after round of ammunition into the defenseless crowd, leaving hundreds dead or wounded. Word of this horrifying clash rapidly spread throughout the country. The bloodbath outraged Iranians, even many of those who had supported the Shah.

I didn't completely understand the reasons for the unrest in the country but, following the events in Tehran, the seriousness of the situation could be sensed even more than before on the streets of Isfahan. It was as if the entire city's colors had been washed away, leaving behind only dark, untold secrets stirring through the silence in the air all around us.

That eerie cold feeling was back inside me.

We all need to respect the power of silence, not only our own, but others, too. Our own silence can calm our spirits and replace our anxieties with tranquility. If we aren't careful, though, others can intentionally use their silence to disquiet our souls. We may be unaware of the effect this has on our spirit because we can't touch it or see it—we can only feel it. The silence is just there, in the air, lingering all around us, pulling at the energy of our spirits. We may feel agitated, uncomfortable, or thrown off balance within our own bodies, allowing the eeriness of others' silence to take hold of our emotions.

Learn to listen, trust, and follow your intuition. Recognize what the silence is telling you. Learn to feel the tugs and pulls on your own body, mind, and spirit. Be aware of the energies within the silence around you, both the good and bad. If necessary, learn to react appropriately to the silence, but do it in your own time, and in your own way, and when it feels right for you. But know you don't have to react to others' silence in any way. You can learn to walk peacefully through the silence around you.

The Bus Ride Home

I T WAS EARLY FALL, THE END of our long bus ride home from school. I was watching out the window a brisk, cool breeze stir autumn leaves on the ground, but as the bus made its routine stop at the end of our *koche*, I noticed something out of the ordinary on the street. Gathered on each side of the *koche* were groups of Iranian boys, including Jaffar, our neighbor. Three dozen or so boys—ranging from around age eight to age seventeen—some wore white bands wrapped around their heads. It looked as if they were just standing around and hanging out. But, when Vance and I stepped off the bus, the boys quickly formed a line on each side of the *koche*. A deafening silence lingered in the air as the bus driver drove away. We instantly sensed coldness stirring in the boys' hearts as they glared at us with piercing stares. As we began to make our way through the center of the two lines, Jaffar suddenly shouted at us in Farsi. We didn't understand him. Jaffar motioned for the rest of the boys to repeat after him. Starting slowly, and then bursting into a fierce, rhythmic chant, the boys shouted over and over again in broken English, "Yank-ee-go-home! Yank-ee-go-home! Yank-ee-go-home!"

With our heads turned to the ground, we quickened our pace toward home, trying to appear calm so the boys wouldn't sense our fear. Our home was only half a block away, but it seemed like miles. By the time we reached our front door my legs felt like rubber. Vance opened the door, and then quickly slammed it. Fumbling with the bolt lock, he secured the door behind us. Stunned, at what had happened, we looked at each other, speechless. Then we both took a deep breath and sighed with relief when we realized how lucky we were to be safely at home.

What we experienced that day was no game, it was real, and it was racism. Vance and I understood this with all certainty. The bitterness toward Americans was very much alive in the Iranian boys' hearts. We could see it in their eyes and sense it in their presence. Their hatred was undeniable.

Oddly, though, I felt no bitterness toward the boys. I knew deep in my heart that the words they chanted weren't their own. These were the words of others that had hardened the boys' hearts against Americans.

After that day, I often questioned why someone would fill innocent minds with such hatred. Who turned the boys' hearts against us? Who taught the boys to hate us because of the color of our skin and birthplace? Who were those people who taught hatred above love and acceptance?

How easy forming a judgment about our brothers and sisters can be from the clothes they wear and the color of their skin. Yes, clothes have a purpose; they protect our bodies, keep us warm, and give us human dignity. And the color of our skin tells the story of our heritage. But neither tells the story of the person inside.

I often wonder how much better a place the world would be if we could all—at least once—walk the streets blind, with our soul visible on the outside. Thus revealing who we are beneath the layers of garments we place on ourselves. If this were possible, where would we go to know who a person is? There would be no place for us to go, but straight to their soul.

Our physical being can create barriers that separate us from our brothers and sisters by religion, social status, and nationality. But, our physical being doesn't have to create barriers. If we could look beyond the visual layers that block our acceptance of one another, we could see that, beneath it all, we're all human beings. We're all vulnerable and we all have the same basic needs. We each have a heart with blood flowing through it, a heart that beats to the rhythm of life. We share the same air and our spirits have the same purpose: to share our personal experience of God's love with all those we meet.

If we all wore our souls on the outside, who would you be? And, if you were blind, what would you see within each soul you meet?

Look beyond the visual layers that might repress your acceptance of others. Open your heart and your spirit to the world. Through this you'll help our world become a better place by being one more spirit reflecting love and harmony in a world where the bond we share with others comes not from the color of our skin, but from the color of our souls.

MY BIRTHDAY

"HAPPY BIRTHDAY TO YOU, Happy Birthday to you, Happy Birthday, dear Tammy, Happy Birthday to you." The melody of the birthday song rang throughout the house. This was my eighteenth birthday. I couldn't believe it, eighteen! And what a surprise everyone remembered my birthday with all the chaos going on outside.

Ed and Nancy gave me a charm with a real tiger's claw encased in gold, which they purchased during our summer vacation in Thailand. Vance handed me a small box. As I opened it, three glittering, handcrafted, eighteen-carat gold bangle bracelets came tumbling out. Tiny cresent moons, stars, and paisley symbols were stamped on the thin bands. These were exactly like the gold bracelets Persian women wore beneath their chadors, layered in rows up their arms, jingling and jangling when they moved their hands.

From the corner of my eye, where Shawn and Damon had been standing, I noticed Shawn had disappeared. But it wasn't long before he returned with a big grin on his face and carrying my birthday present. Looking up all I could see was my orange reflection in the giant, hammered copper teakettle I'd been admiring for months. Later, Shawn said he'd decided to take on the copper merchant and try to make a deal but, with the animosity growing toward Americans, the shopkeeper wouldn't

185

budge from his price. Shawn broke down and bought the teakettle for me anyway, paying the full price.

Damon explained he'd bought me a cute little trinket for my birthday, but, as he walked alone down Hafez street from the bazaar, a mob of young men began pursuing him, working their way into a frenzy, taunting and shouting out to him, "Yankee go home! Yankee go home!" As the mob moved closer, Damon quickened his pace and, accidentally, dropped the trinket and it shattered all over the ground. Uncertain if he was going to make it home safely, he didn't dare look back to survey the damage. He just kept on walking faster and faster.

The Candy man, who happened to witness the hostility, quickly motioned for Damon to take refuge inside his shop. As Damon stepped inside, the merchant immediately pulled down his metal gate and locked it. The Candy man sheltered Damon until the mob finally settled down and disappeared down the road. Then, unlocking the gate, he motioned for Damon to leave quickly and be on his way home. From the *koche* corner, the Candy man watched Damon until he saw him safely slip inside our front door. Damon said, after that frightening experience, he didn't have time to get another present. So he and Shawn decided to share Shawn's gift, and, together, they gave me the teakettle.

Shawn and Damon decided we would all celebrate my birthday with a "little" tea, so off they went to the kitchen to fill the teakettle with water. We soon heard them coming back from the kitchen laughing hysterically. When they entered the living room, we all laughed too, as we watched water pouring from all the broken seams in the copper teakettle. Only then did we question our vulnerability for believing the shopkeeper's claims of honesty and the promise that his craftsmanship was nothing less than the best.

But I didn't mind that the teakettle wasn't perfect. It was still just as charming to me as it was the first day I noticed it shining on Copper Alley. In fact, the copper teakettle was the perfect gift for me.

The copper teakettle now sits on my kitchen counter in front of the sink. I leave it there to remind me of a time gone by, a time of rain and sunshine. It reminds me of where I've been and what I've seen. It reminds me of what I've felt. It reflects my life like a mirror.

I love to surround myself with things that inspire me and bring color, character, charm, and beauty into my world. Try surrounding yourself with things that inspire you and remind you of how far you've come, how far you can go, and what you've seen. Try surrounding yourself with whatever is in this life that brightens your world, lifts your spirit, and brings back special memories.

Although our memories seem to fade with time, our souls don't fade. Our souls hold on to the light of what has surrounded us in this life. Even when we forget why we believe a certain way or what brought us to a certain belief, our soul doesn't forget. Because our soul is who we are, it reflects our life like a mirror.

My copper teakettle is a little tarnished now. It seems to age with me, yet it's still there to reflect on, just as all the memories. So, don't hesitate to surprise someone with a special gift. You never know what memories it will keep alive, deep inside his or her soul.

THE DARK SPACE

I strengthened my ears, struggling to hear the muffled sound in the distance more clearly. A great commotion seemed to be coming from the Grand Bazaar or possibly the Royal Mosque, several blocks away. Listening even harder, the sound seemed to be intensifying. I began to feel small vibrations run beneath my feet. The commotion was getting closer, the vibrations stronger, and the noise louder and louder, and much more intense. I realized what I was listening to must be thousands of Iranians, marching and chanting down Hafez Street. As the demonstrators' powerful voices filled the air, a terrifying chill rippled though me. I felt the hatred that was raging in their hearts run through my body. As they moved down the street, their bitter, angry words became crystal clear. Over and over, they shouted in a slow, rhythmic chant of mixed Farsi and broken English: "Down with Carter! Down with the Shah! Down with Carter! Down with the Shah!"

The deafening words made my head throb. I placed my hands over my ears, trying to silence the sound. The Earth's trembles turned to rumbles under my feet when I realized the mob of demonstrators was being led down the *koche* in front of our house. Fear overwhelmed me. We were living in the heart of the Islamic community. There was nowhere for me to go, no refuge beyond the mud walls. *Where's Heather?* I thought. I panicked.

I'd last seen Heather playing in the courtyard. I spun around to search for her.

Looking through the glass in the French doors, I saw her standing there by the fountain, her fire-red hair and innocent freckled face staring back at me. Her big blue eyes were filled with tears. As if in slow motion, I ran to her, swept her up in my arms, and then raced to the secret room built beneath the floor. I quickly lifted Heather in, climbed in, nestled my way into the cramped space, and then closed the door behind us. The thunderous sound of rolling chants and marching feet pounded against the mud walls surrounding us. The noise was too loud to tell if any of the demonstrators had entered our house.

As we settled into the cold, dark, hiding place, Heather began to whimper. I held my hand lightly over her mouth. Trembling, I tried to reassure her that everything would be okay. "We just need to be very, very quiet and still for a while. Later, you can go back outside and play," I told her. But my heart was pounding from the force of the fear that I felt. I knew it was possible for the demonstrators to scale the mud walls, climb onto the rooftop, jump into the courtyard, and find us hiding there.

Not knowing what to do next, I closed my eyes and cuddled Heather tightly in my arms. I hoped and prayed the sounds would go away. At that moment, I began to wonder if I would ever see my family again. I promised God and myself that, if I did, I would shower them with love and always let them know how much I cherish them.

Then, out of the blue, a picture of the peasant lady Erica and I saw on our way to the pool that summer surfaced from the back of my mind. The woman's image took over my imagination. I saw myself emerge from under a tattered chador, pretending to be deaf and dumb, while I hid from Islamic extremists on the streets of Isfahan.

That's it! I thought. If necessary, I would live on the streets, pretending to be a beggar until Ed found us or until I found Mr. Mosepore or someone else to help us find a way out of Iran. As these imaginary thoughts raced though my mind and the answer became clearer about what I could do next, calmness replaced my fear. I realized I could do something if it became necessary. I didn't have to wait there in fear; I could take some control of my destiny.

Only forty-five minutes or so had passed, but this seemed like a lifetime. I noticed the chants and sounds of marching feet were gradually fading away into the distance, just as they had begun. Not knowing if it were safe to come out yet, I cracked open the door of our secret hiding place to see daylight. When I looked around, the only trace left of the hatred raging in the demonstrators' hearts was the shattered remnants of a blown-up Molotov cocktail lying on the ground near the courtyard fountain.

I often wonder about the peasant woman who quieted my fear that day and how each person who enters our life has a purpose. That purpose may be to feed our spirits by inspiring us in ways we could never imagine. I wonder if the cloud I imagined following her on that hot summer day wasn't a cloud at all. Maybe it was a halo. And, possibly, the shame and humiliation I thought I saw was nothing more than the humility of an angel. In an instant, the peasant woman lifted my fear and showed me that I did have some control over my destiny. Where

would I have turned to comfort my fears if our paths hadn't crossed on the street that day?

Some try to place fear in our minds, yet others are there to take it away. The peasant woman guided me through my fears. She guided me to a calmer state without ever knowing the effect her presence had on my life that frightening, cold winter day.

Popcorn Seeds

HEATHER AND I WERE ENJOYING a bowl of fresh popcorn as we watched cartoons after school. I heard "crunch, crunch" and realized Heather was chewing on the unpopped kernels she picked from the bottom of the popcorn bowl.

"Heather, don't eat the seeds," I scolded.

Looking up at me, a little confused, she asked, "Why? I like the seeds."

"I like them too, Heather, but they'll crack your teeth."

Satisfied with my answer, she quit munching on the popcorn seeds. Unfortunately, I didn't. A few minutes later, I felt a crumble inside my mouth. I'd cracked one of my lower teeth while biting an unpopped kernel.

Nancy made a dentist appointment to get my tooth fixed the next day. The idea of going to an Iranian dentist had never crossed my mind, and after entering his office and looking around, I wasn't sure I wanted to be there, let alone have him work on my tooth.

A strong aroma of sandalwood drifted through the dimly lit work area. A small table decorated with artificial pink roses held a brass burner, from which incense smoldered. The office was a bit dusty and the instruments looked neither shiny nor clean; in fact, they looked like they'd been designed in the early 1900s. But my tooth hurt and needed to be fixed, and Nancy reassured me that Dr. Ramazani was a good dentist.

So, there I sat, in an old, worn-out, brown leather dental chair, my mouth wide-open, with Dr. Ramazani's bushy, black beard brushing against my cheek as he examined my tooth with a tiny mirror. Dr. Ramazani didn't use any Novocain to stop the pain. He carefully drilled and grinded on my tooth, while calmly talking to me in broken English. It was only my concentration on what he was trying to say that distracted my attention and lessened the pain.

I didn't know what Dr. Ramazani used to fill my tooth with that day, but the tooth never felt quite the same. My tooth was a little rough on top and my mouth felt heavy on the right side, as if a lead weight was pulling down that side of my mouth.

Occasionally we try to warn others of the outcome of their actions. We try to give them advice as we continue to do exactly what we warned them about. We may tell a friend that a situation is unhealthy for them, while our own situation is unhealthy too.

But, someday, we may be confronted with our false colors. Someday, if we don't listen to our own conscience and take our own advice, we may have to live with the outcome of our actions.

We should all strive to live our lives through example, by reflecting our hearts true colors through our bodies actions, because these colors can never be realized by others solely through our words.

Dusk Curfew

I N EARLY DECEMBER A DUSK-TO-DAWN curfew was officially declared and stringently enforced throughout Iran. Even though the entire country had been placed under martial law, the battle for power over the nation's future continued to escalate. The overthrow of Muhammad Reza Shah by Ayatollah Khomeini's followers looked inevitable. American flags, and pictures of President Carter and the Shah, went up in flames as university students in major cities went on rampages through the streets discharging firebombs, shattering windows, and ransacking businesses.

In Isfahan, we watched as Iranian soldiers heavily patrolled the streets. Armored trucks and tanks were strategically placed throughout the town to control the erupting demonstrations against the Shah's government. Throughout Iran, the Shah's secret police, *Savak,* were rumored to have raided businesses, homes, and mosques trying to stop the uprisings by arresting government opposition leaders. The media ground to a halt and doors to many government buildings—including universities and schools—were slammed shut and locked. But none of these restrictions seemed to stop the powerful Islamic clergymen and their followers from trying to erode the Shah's authority.

Many wealthy bazaar merchants, who had economical motives, as well as political and religious convictions for removing the Shah from power, helped fund the clergy's fanatical uprising. Throughout

Iran, bazaars and mosques were being used as political platforms and underground meeting places to coordinate demonstrations against the government. Audio tape recordings of the exiled Ayatollah Khomeini preaching anti-Shah propaganda and pro-Islamic fundamentalism were used to strengthen the clergy's position against the government. And mass gatherings of townspeople and villagers who patronized the Islamic mosques were used to build the necessary amount of animosity, momentum, and manpower needed to overthrow Muhammad Reza Pahlavi as the king of Iran.

Day after day we watched as the Shah's military restraints against the Islamic revolt virtually unraveled. By mid December, the mullahs' fanatical views of Islamic doctrine had penetrated the soul of the nation, creating a passionate outrage against the Shah within the hearts of many Iranian people.

The defiant mullahs would stop at nothing to bring back the exiled Ayatollah Khomeini from France for their cause of forcing the "good" of Islamic traditions back on to all Iranian people—non-Muslims and Muslims alike. These were many of the same traditions the Shah and his father, the king before him, had gradually stripped away as they forced modernization and the "good" from the western world, particularly America, into Persian culture. As the two Pahlavi kings, one after the other, integrated modernization into Iran's culture, they lost sight of the country's Zoroastrian, Persian, and Islamic identity. But, after decades in power, Muhammad Reza Shah's great emphasis on America is what ultimately outraged the majority of disenchanted Iranians. Rather than the king simply respecting America for what it was, he wanted to reproduce America's image within Iran's borders and, to do so, meant turning his back on many of Iran's ancient traditions and its historical past.

The revolution of a country torn among the western world, Persian culture, and Islam was unfolding before our eyes. We watched, waited, and hoped for an end to the chaos, but the end was nowhere in sight.

For whatever reason, some people want to repress other people. They want us to believe they hold our future in their hands. They want to take control of our lives and force us to be who they want. They want to tell us who we are, what to do, how to dress, how to act, how to live our lives, and what to believe. They want control and sometimes will stop at nothing to force their ways on us. We need to ask ourselves, "Do these people really care about us? Or, do they care only about themselves and their own beliefs?"

Recognize control for what is—repression—repression of the mind, the body and the spirit. Be wary of people who tell you they know the only way and, without them, a good life is impossible. These people, if allowed, will take our freedom away, sometimes by force and sometimes so slowly, we don't even realize our freedom has been taken away.

But we don't have to accept others' beliefs as if they were true in our own minds and hearts. We don't have to relinquish our spirit or our freedom and live our life through others' eyes.

Break free from the control of others that is disguised as protection or security. Break free from those who say,

"I'm doing this for your own good." Someone else's idea of good does not need to be forced on you. You instinctively know what is good. Trust your own instincts and follow your own heart. Believe in yourself, knowing that you have the right and the responsibility to control your own life.

SHOTS IN THE NIGHT

OFF AND ON THROUGHOUT THE COLD nights, we could hear mobs of Iranian men near our home, shouting in protest of the Shah's regime. Before long, sporadic shots of gunfire broke out, discharged from armed soldiers patrolling the moonlit streets. Then, suddenly, nothing. The noise stopped. The city lay silent.

Night after night, the sound of crackling bullets echoing over our courtyard walls sent chills running down my spine. I curled up tightly and sank deeper into bed. Frightened, I'd lie still with my eyes open wide late into the night. Then, somewhere in the rain of fire and silence, I'd slowly give in to my body's need for rest, close my eyes, and fall asleep.

Ed reassured us that the clashes at night weren't as bad as they sounded. And he said the shots discharged by the Iranian soldiers were probably only blanks used to intimidate pro-Khomeini demonstrators into conforming. I couldn't help wonder, though, if Ed was only trying to protect us from our fear by giving us the assurance we needed. Yet, Ed's poise and confidence is what finally reassured us that we did have some control over our future.

Others may stop at nothing to manipulate us with fear. They may hold an imaginary gun to our heads, showing us they have the ability to dictate our lives and tell us if we don't conform or follow them, terrible things will happen. These people take away our dignity and intentionally erode our self-confidence by ensuring the fear they place in us will oppress our spirit. They try to take our freedom away by reminding us that they have the power to control our fate.

These people don't understand that they can't hold the whole world in the palm of their hands and force life to happen the way they choose. They don't understand that life isn't intended to be lived through a sense of fear. If these people could only understand the power they truly hold in the palm of their hands. They hold the power of love, which is more powerful than fear could ever be.

If it seems someone is holding a gun to your head, quietly remove this illusion from your mind. Believe in yourself and your own ability to control your life. Then have the self-confidence to stand by your belief.

ED'S SILHOUETTE

VANCE LOVED TO VENTURE OFF ALONE to the bazaar, where he sometimes spent hours bargaining with the merchants. One unusually calm and quiet morning as Vance wandered through the marketplace—completely oblivious to the mood and what was happening around him—an old bazaar merchant that he had bartered with many times before shouted at him, "You must go now! Run fast!" while nodding his head and pointing toward the mosque at the other end of Shah's Square. Vance knew immediately why the merchant was so concerned for his safety as he turned to witness thousands of pro-Khomeini and anti-American-Shah demonstrators gathering for an uprising. All the merchants began closing their shops, for they knew the demonstrators' course of action was unpredictable. Heeding the old man's advice, Vance took off running as fast as he could toward home. Metal gates slammed behind him as he raced down Hafez Street. Frightened and breathless, he entered our front door to safety, forever grateful to the old man who had forewarned him of the uprising.

Animosity and the episodes of hostility against us rapidly increased. One late afternoon, we returned home from visiting with our British friends to find our front door charred and still smoldering from someone's attempt to burn down our house. Lucky for us, and the entire neighborhood, the fire died out before it did any real damage. Ed said that after decades of repeated painting the flames probably couldn't penetrate through the many layers of thick paint.

Early one morning, Vance and I woke to some commotion in front of our house. We peeked over the rooftop, and watched as Ed and Kurt tried to grasp hold of the fact that someone had flipped over our jeep during the night. The jeep was lying in the middle of the *koche,* blocking the path of morning commuters. The small crowds of Iranian men gathered around the car were just as surprised as we were to see the jeep turned over. Mustering up as many muscles as possible, the guys and several sympathetic Iranians returned the jeep to its upright position. Ed thanked the men for their help, and then turned to enter our house, only to see the words "Yankee-go-home" boldly written over our charred green door in bright red spray paint.

As the aggression grew, the issue of our safety became a genuine concern, especially since our home was buried in the heart of the Islamic community with no safeguards against the Muslim extremists' hostility. Ed knew we were no longer safe on the streets or in our home. Our freedom was being taken away and replaced with fear.

That evening, dressed in full military Army greens, laced up black boots, and an Army cap, Ed bravely walked through the house, up the stairs, and through the side door in Kurt's bedroom that led outside on to the rooftop. There, in the chilly night, Ed began to stand guard with the silhouette shape of a gun he had carved from a piece of wood as his only protection. Squatting down on the rooftop beneath the moonlight, he watched over the *koche* below, hoping the reflection of his silhouette would ward off any more hostility against us.

Silly as this may seem, knowing Ed was on the rooftop, watching guard over us at night, gave me a sense of security. I could finally close my eyes and fall asleep.

Ed was a brave man. He risked his life to protect his family. He warded off others who may have been there to harm us. With his silhouette, he protected us from further danger.

I often see others place an imaginary shield around them, as if they need to create an armored guard to protect themselves from danger. But they do this when the world around them is at peace. They close others out of their lives by repressing their true spirit.

These people may have been hurt in the past and they may believe the only way to protect themselves from pain is to wear invisible armor. They often do this without even realizing the penetrating effect this has on their lives. And, often, the very thing they guard themselves against is what they need to experience and to see, or it's the very thing they need to let go of in their hearts to be free from the danger they perceive.

Sometimes we need to have the courage to let down our guard and make ourselves vulnerable enough to face the world outside, to discover what really makes us secure and at peace in our lives. Because an armored shield in times of peace only guards us against the freedom we truly need to be safe and secure—freedom of the spirit.

The Commute to Work

Despite the turmoil around us, Ed, Nancy, and Shawn continued to work, leaving each morning at daybreak, although they always took extra precautions not to draw attention to themselves on their daily commutes. Shawn wore a hat and a wool scarf wrapped around his neck to cover his fair complexion and light brown hair. Nancy wore baggy pants, a large overcoat, and a silk scarf draped over her hair and tied beneath her chin. Ed, with his dark hair and olive complexion, simply blended in.

Their commutes became a confusing struggle as the three tried to drive through the city to reach the American base on the outskirts of town. They didn't know from one morning to the next what to expect from angry Iranian mobs gathered along the sidewalks and street corners, or whose political side they should proclaim they were on.

But Ed and Nancy knew they would need to show a picture of devotion for either the Shah or Khomeini, depending on which day or street corner the mobs stopped them. To insure they wouldn't get harmed or the car windshield wouldn't get smashed from hammers, rocks, or sticks the angry mobs waved and threatened with, Ed and Nancy began to carry two photographs—one of the Shah and one of Khomeini. Flashing one or the other picture to satisfy that particular faction, they could safely continue on their way to work, unharmed and with the car in one piece.

Over and over, we could hear, feel and see that the nation's soul was out of sync but stuck in the middle, all we could do was to go with the flow and move peacefully through the obstacles around us.

From time to time we may find ourselves stuck in the middle of a situation through no fault of our own. And all we can do at the moment is to continue on peacefully until we find our way and what's right for us. So try to be patient when life becomes confusing, when you don't know which path is safe. Sometimes you just need to go with the flow until the answer comes to lead you out of harm's way.

PART NINE

THE JOURNEY HOME

How
Did the rose
Ever open its heart

And give to this world
All its
Beauty?

It felt the encouragement of light
Against its
Being,

Otherwise,
We all remain

Too

Frightened.

—Hafiz, from The Gift

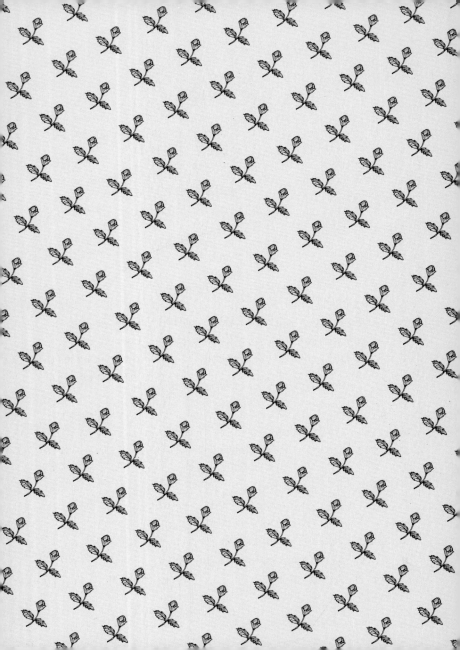

DALE'S YARD SALE

O NE SATURDAY AFTERNOON, Vance, Damon, and I were hanging out with a few friends at Dale's apartment located in a partially developed district, sprawling outward near the city's desert edge. Shawn joined us, a little perplexed, yet amused as he began to recount his experience of purchasing gas on the way to Dale's place.

Rumors had rapidly spread that oil workers had gone on strike in defiance of the Shah. As a result, the lines at gas stations all over town had quickly grown to several blocks long. Rumor had it that the country was going to run out of oil, so many people frantically began hoarding what fuel they could. Despite the seriousness of the situation, it did seem ironic that one of the most oil-rich countries in the world was in the midst of an oil shortage.

Dale took the situation a little more serious than Shawn and the rest of us. Conditions all over the city were rapidly deteriorating. Dale predicted the oil shortage would be the final straw before an emergency notice was issued from the U.S. Embassy to evacuate all Americans from the country.

On the spur of the moment, Dale decided he was going to have a yard sale and clear out some of his belongings, but the thought never seemed to cross his mind that he didn't have a yard as he began gathering up the stuff he wanted to sell. Besides lots of odds and ends, the items included worn-out tennis shoes, old jeans and T-shirts, some musical equipment, and a few radios in poor working condition. We watched Dale through a window as he placed the useless items on the dirt in front of the iron gate entrance to his home. Propping up a makeshift For Sale sign behind the stuff, Dale stepped back for a moment waiting for his yard sale to kick off.

Two village men walking past the apartment abruptly stopped, and then stood back a little, eyeballing what Dale had placed on the ground. Curious, they stepped a little closer as if they were trying to understand what the strange gesture was all about. As they grasped what was happening, the men moved closer to examine the second-hand goods more carefully. Cautiously, the men picked up a radio, and then began inspecting it from all sides. We could see an expression of fascination grow across their faces as they began turning the knobs, and checking out the electric cords and wires. What we experienced from that moment on convinced us that Dale's yard sale was the first-ever yard sale in Iran.

A couple of boys approached Dale's sale. Both were wearing headbands like the boys wore at the bus stop. These headbands signified the boys' willingness to become martyrs for Islam. But death seemed the last thing on their minds when they spotted Dale's old stereo lying on the ground. As the boys walked away with their prized possession, several other people came along, quickly grabbing up different items, and then offering Dale money. Within minutes, Dale yelled for the guys in the house to come outside and help him negotiate prices with the people.

Word of the sale had spread through the entire neighborhood and, before we knew it, fifty or so Iranians had popped-up from out of nowhere and were standing at the front gate wanting to buy something—anything that was American and electronic. Dale was quickly running out of things to sell, but the demand for American goods was soaring. The situation intensified as people started yelling, reaching, and grabbing at anything, even trying to buy the clothes the guys were wearing. At that point, we all realized the situation was getting completely out-of-hand, so the guys slowly worked their way back behind the entrance gate, and then closed and locked it behind them for safety. There, they continued to sell the few remaining items through gaps between the gate's metal bars until, finally, nothing was left.

When Dale told the people the yard sale was over, some became irritated, frantically reaching through the gaps while shaking the gate. In fear that they'd started a small riot, the guys withdrew from the situation by retreating back inside the house. After a long wait, the mob finally broke up and disappeared down the road, leaving us all relieved yet a little shaken.

We can never predict the exact outcome of a given situation, yet we still need to practice clear thought. We all need to be spontaneous at times—it's exhilarating, it refreshes our mind, and it frees our spirit. Just for a while, it gives us a break from the repetitious world we live in, allowing us to let go and have some fun.

But even when we have the urge to do something on a whim, we need to think with a clear conscience as to what the outcome of our actions could bring. We can't always follow our impulses alone; we need to use common sense too.

Sometimes the action just doesn't fit the circum-stances around us. It's all in the mood, situation, place, and timing. Sometimes no matter how much money, fun, or excitement we think our actions might bring, the unknown outcome isn't worth the risk of wounding our spirits or endangering our lives.

Think clearly, even when you feel the need to react spontaneously. If things don't turn out the way you planned, back away—before it's too late, before the situation gets out of hand, before it pulls you in and leaves your spirit shaken.

FRIENDS

OUR IRANIAN NEIGHBORS ACROSS the *koche* were always gracious and friendly to us, but late in December, they reluctantly told Ed and Nancy they could no longer allow their two children—Hommad and Monzulia—to play with Heather. Faced with the ever-increasing animosity toward Americans, by no fault of their own, the parents feared their children's friendship with Heather could place their young son and daughter in danger.

The three children had been inseparable, constantly crossing the *koche* and knocking on each other's doors to see if one or the other could go outside and play. They talked, pretended, and giggled, just as most children do. Monzulia often freed her little arms by throwing her chador behind her back as the three children squatted in the *koche* or the courtyard inspecting tiny bugs. Then the two girls, deeming a bug yucky, would plead for Hommad to smash it with his rubber sandals, which, like most little boys, he did gladly.

At the ripe old ages of four, five, and six, none of the children understood the seriousness of the political situation around them. All the children knew was they could no longer play together. But the new boundaries placed on them didn't prevent them from smiling, giggling, and waving to each other, while sneaking peeks across the *koche* from their front doors. This went on until Monzulia and Hommad's mother, draped in her black chador, came along, scolded her children for socializing with Heather, and then quickly shut their door. It wasn't long, though, before the doors were flung back open and the three children were once again playing their new game.

To the children, nothing could take their playmates away. It was too late, for their pure hearts had innocently touched and formed a bond of simple love through friendship.

Others may try to place boundaries on us to prevent our friendships from flourishing. But through all the discouragement and the disenchanting events in life, a true friend still stands. They lift and strengthen our spirits with an understanding heart, a gentle hand, a warm smile, a sweet embrace, an honest or thoughtful word, and an open door.

A true friend offers us a home in their heart forever. A true friend protects us and gives our spirit a safe place to dwell in the world. A true friend always finds a way to share their love, no matter what the obstacles may be. A true friend is there to stay no matter what others say. A true friendship has no boundaries—only endless love, faith, promise, and possibilities. A true friend opens the door to their heart with love, hope, and security.

A Passion for Persia

MARTIAL LAW AND THE DUSK curfew were still in effect and several months had passed since Americans were told to keep a low profile throughout Iran. Ed looked exhausted from his routine of working during the day and standing guard on the rooftop at night. Shawn began to rotate turns with him, squatting on the rooftop, watching guard over the *koche,* while Ed slept.

Pictures of Khomeini began to replace pictures of the Shah in merchants' shops. American flags, and pictures of President Carter and the Shah, continued to go up in flames during sporadic uprisings. The sound of marching feet and rhythmic chants could be heard on almost a daily basis. The American School of Isfahan extended Christmas vacation until further notice, while rumor spread of the United States evacuating all American women and children from Iran.

We anxiously waited for new word from Mr. Mosepore and our Muslim friends—Hammond and Goat-Goat—about what was whispered on the streets. Our friends were as saddened as we were about what was happening in their country. They didn't want Khomeini to come into power and force their country into a rigid Islamic-controlled nation. They didn't want what freedom they had taken away. But our friends believed they could do nothing to stop the unrest, for Khomeini had amassed a faithful following that was too strong to stop. Our friends believed they could only stand back and watch the transformation of their country unfold, as the unyielding mullahs continued to instigate any activities that weakened the Shah's power.

The majority of Iranians wanted to merge with the modern world, but they wanted to do so in their own time and in their own way, not in the time and the ways forced on them by the nation's government. For years, the Shah ignored ordinary Iranian voices about what was best for Iran and its people. He seemed to listen to only those voices from the western world, leaving the door wide open for Islamic fundamentalist beliefs—beliefs that, in the end, could dominate the liberties of the Iranian people and quietly take hold of the nation.

We began to hear stories of many well-educated and affluent Iranian families fleeing the country they loved out of fear of the Islamic regime. They took with them their knowledge, their vast wealth, and a few worldly possessions.

We were in the midst of a revolution, living among extraordinarily self-sufficient and intelligent people who seemed to be frantically grasping for a sense of balance and a fresh identity from within the world around them. An identity not drawn from the western world but, instead, from their own Persian history and religious faiths.

Many of these people were going so far as to allow Ayatollah Khomeini's literal interpretation of the Qur'an to control their way of life. This was an interpretation that seemed to have little to do with the natural progress of the country or the dignity and freedom of the people. Instead, it seemed only to do with the Ayatollah and his followers' fanatical religious doctrine. But many Iranian people so desperately wanted to hold on to their twenty-five hundred year-old Persian culture and Islamic identity that they took hold of Khomeini's rigid ideology because, at that time, they found no other light to hold on to within Iran's leaders.

It was as if deep within the soul of the country, all the people truly wanted was a certain respect and acceptance of their ancient civilization from the outside world. Understandably, they believed they were worthy of such respect because of their extraordinary place in human history.

Iran was a nation divided, literally torn between the new and the old way of life. The threads that intertwined the Persian culture together were much more complex than we understood. The Islamic extremist's passion was unlike any passion I'd ever seen. Their entire being was thrust into their beliefs. Their passion was woven into their hearts and souls with the same passion that the Persian carpets were woven through their hands. And, as we watched the fearful events intensify all around us, it become more and more apparent that the country's unrest had only just begun to unfold.

I often wonder how much better our world would be if we all had the kind of passion the Iranians had that caused them to stand by their beliefs. Many of us see injustice alive in the world every day. But we often stand back and watch injustice take place because we don't want to get caught up in a complicated situation from fear of what the repercussions for getting involved may have on our lives. Often we turn our back and walk the other way in fear, because we don't have enough courage and passion to follow our own conscience and heart.

But the only fear we should carry with us is the fear of justice, love, and freedom diminishing in our world. If we truly believe in the power of justice, love, and freedom, we will insure these are never taken away through the influence, narrow-mindedness, or control of others. We will express our own passion to life through our artistic gifts, our words and, if necessary, through our actions.

Find your true passion in life. Let it reflect who you are. Let it reflect your intolerance to a world deficient in justice, love, and freedom, even if this means challenging authority. You never know—this could help change a life, a country, or the world.

WAITING FOR NEWS

THE CITY'S ELECTRICITY, TELEPHONE lines, and water were intermittently cut off throughout the day and night, interrupting our daily routine and blocking us from any communication with the outside world. Fortunately, we had Ed's old battery-operated transistor radio, which sometimes picked up the fuzzy reception spoken over the British Broadcasting Company (BBC).

Iranian radio and television news broadcasts were carefully controlled, excluding any information of the nation's unrest. Most days, the television news was replaced all together with cartoons or old movies, so we carefully listened for any objective news reported over the static waves of the BBC. We eagerly waited to hear what the rest of the world was saying about the unrest in Tehran, because we knew whatever happened on the streets of the country's capital, whether good or bad, would soon find its way to Isfahan and other major cities throughout the nation.

To find our way through the house at night, we lit candles and, to pass the time away and keep our minds off the unrest outside, we played cards, charades, or backgammon under the flickering candlelight. All we could do was wait, and then bundle up under our warm blankets and fall asleep to the sound of sporadic gunfire echoing through the clear, cold nights.

At times we make ourselves crazy by trying to learn the outcome of a situation before it happens. We try to peek around the corner into the future. But, sometimes, there is nothing we can do but stay informed by the means available, and then wait.

Now and again, we have little control over the events in our lives. And when we try to control the process of the experience, this only makes us become more uptight, frustrated, and anxious. Sometimes we simply need to leave the future alone and find something to occupy our minds. We'll feel much more at peace if we can relax and appreciate the moment, since we never really know what the next moment will bring.

So try to let the lessons of life unfold gracefully, try to let life simply happen, since that's what will transpire anyway.

And while you are waiting, try to keep in mind that tomorrow will be another day; the sun will shine again. The answer to what you've been waiting for will come.

LETTING GO OF DREAMS

VANCE AND I BELIEVED THAT music blaring from the vendors' shops would soon liven up the streets again. And haggling merchants, happy to see Americans, would once again show their welcoming smiles, gesturing for us to step into their shops and browse around. We sincerely believed all the turmoil would soon fade away, and then we could carry on with our plans in Isfahan.

I had so much to look forward to, such as my high school graduation ceremony from Toufanian High School and all the great jobs available with American companies after I received my diploma. I looked forward to our family trip, migrating with Mr. Mosepore and the Bakhtiyar tribe to the mountains outside Isfahan. But, above all, I looked forward to learning more about the history, the culture, and the people of Iran. There was so much left to do and see, there was so much left to learn, it was as if our journey was ending when it had only just begun.

One afternoon, Vance and Heather were riding our bicycle home after buying some sweets at the candy shop when a robust, old woman approached them near our front door. Just as Vance lifted Heather off the handlebars, the woman, fully clad in her black chador began shaking her finger and yelling at him in Farsi. Vance didn't understand what the woman had said, but she was obviously upset and angry. Despite her youth, Heather spoke Farsi fluently, so Vance asked her to translate what the woman had said. Heather looked up at Vance and whispered, "She said, you American, you die." With Heather at his side, Vance entered the house, troubled by what had happened. He couldn't believe an innocent old woman could say such a cold-hearted, terrorizing thing.

Even though Vance and I didn't want to leave Isfahan, the reality of what was happening all around us was too glaring to ignore. We finally realized that no matter how much we wanted to stay and watch the season change, the chaos wasn't going to end soon. The wounds from the western world had cut too deeply into the core of Persian culture. The majority of the Iranians couldn't find any light coming from within the Americans to hold onto. The bitterness raging in the people's hearts was just too strong to stop. It was as if only time and distance from the western world would bring peace to the people's souls.

We often resist and deny the changes we need in our lives that are necessary to continue on our journey. We may not want our situation to change, so we resist and deny that things are the way they really are. We prolong the inevitable by looking the other way, pretending what we see isn't the reality at the time.

But, sooner or later, we must face the truth. We have to say, "This is the way it is, whether I want to see it this way or not. I can no longer deny it. I can no longer resist the truth because the truth is right there in front of me, whether I like it or not."

At times, it may take a while for our minds to absorb

the reality of this truth. We may resist and deny the truth until it's time for our hearts to accept it. We finally come to realize, that we must let go when we have no light to hold onto or to give. But this doesn't mean the light won't shine again as our passage through life goes on.

Hammond, Goat-Goat, and Mr. Mosepore

MR. MOSEPORE WAS LEAVING OUR home just as Hammond and Goat-Goat were pulling up in Goat-Goat's blue BMW. The sound of Persian music pounded against the car's rolled-up windows. Even though Mr. Mosepore, Hammond, and Goat-Goat were all our family friends, their paths had never crossed in our home before that day.

Hammond and Goat-Goat were best friends—one was nineteen years old and the other was twenty. Both were raised in affluent Iranian families, where they enjoyed high social status and material things, both of which were important to them. Hammond was uncommonly tall and husky for his Iranian ancestry. Goat-Goat was of average height and had a bashful, boyish manner, which complemented Hammond's outspoken and lively charm.

After Mr. Mosepore drove away, Hammond raised his voice in a troubled tone? "Who was that man and what was he doing in your home?" With a big smile, Damon cheerfully answered, "That's Mr. Mosepore, Ed's good friend. He's a philosophy professor at the University of Isfahan. He's a very good man."

Hammond's brows raised and his big brown eyes became incredibly wide as a look of disbelief grew across his face. Then, he snapped abruptly and, shaking his finger, he shouted, "That man is no professor. He's nothing! He's nothing but a doorman at the Khorosh Hotel!"

Hammond was obviously upset at our family's friendship with Mr. Mosepore. At the same time, Damon, Vance, and I were more than a little startled by Hammond's response to Mr. Mosepore's presence in our home. The three of us stood there, looking at each other, not sure what to say to Hammond next. Although we did try to take his words seriously, we couldn't help but chuckle a little beneath our breath over his reaction toward our friend.

As Hammond and Goat-Goat questioned us about Mr. Mosepore's profession, we began to question our friend's occupation ourselves. We wondered if Mr. Mosepore had misled us or if Hammond had mistaken him for someone else.

At times we may judge others by their social status before we truly take time to know them for who they are. Try to envision the world if we were to tear down the walls between wealth and poverty. Envision how much richer a world this would be. We could enjoy someone's companionship simply because we like them for who they are, regardless of their social status.

We never did learn for sure if Mr. Mosepore was a doorman at the Khorosh Hotel or a professor at the university. The answer never came. So, we were all left to wonder, "Did it really matter in the end? Was Mr. Mosepore still our friend?"

Mr. Mosepore taught us about Iranian history, and

introduced us to his family and friends. He invited us into the privacy of his home, and made us feel welcome in his country. He was there in the beginning and he was there at the end, risking his life associating with us. He was our friend.

Maybe we should all take a second look at how we choose our friends, and ask ourselves, "Is this person's social status the reason they are in my life or is it because of their friendship?" Maybe then we will see that wealth doesn't come from what we have but, instead, from what we give away from the richness in our heart.

Time to Leave

Official word finally came down from the American Embassy of the evacuation of all American women and children from Iran. The men would stay behind. In an instant Vance's dreams and mine had vanished. The life we had planned in Isfahan was gone.

Reluctantly, we all packed our belongings. Then, late in the evening of January 6, 1979, all bundled up and weighted down with suitcases, guitars, and rolled-up Persian carpets, we stepped out the front door of our mud house, one by one, into the crisp winter air. Piling both cars high with what belongings we could, we all squeezed into the leftover space in the car seats. Ed drove the Pakyan and, Shawn, the little green Jeep. One car behind the other, they slowly drove us away. The headlights were kept off for our protection, as Ed and Shawn purposely avoided military checkpoints along the way. Not even a *joob* dog roamed through the eerily dark and deserted streets. Only the glow from the moonlight and street lamps filtering through a thin layer of fog lit our way.

Undetected by Islamic rebels or military guards on the streets, we safely arrived at the Khorosh Hotel across town. There, along with the rest of the American dependants living in Isfahan, we were directed to stay for the night by officials of Bell Helicopter and the American Embassy. We were told not to step outside the doors of the hotel until our scheduled departure time in the morning. And, under no circumstances, were we to let Iranians on the streets know Americans were staying there.

Hammond and Goat-Goat couldn't stay away. They wanted to see us one last time to say good-bye. Around three in the morning they finally left the hotel, after partying and laughing it up with the guys all night. But, in the end, tears filled their eyes. They were sad to see their friends go, but they knew we had no other choice.

Ed and Shawn would stay in Isfahan until the evacuation of American men was announced. They would pack the rest of our belongings and ship them to the United States. We didn't want to leave Ed and Shawn behind, but all we could do was hope and pray they'd be safe. At least we had some peace of mind knowing Mr. Mosepore, Hammond, and Goat-Goat, as well as other Iranian and American friends were there to assist them if they needed help.

The experience of watching our dreams come to an abrupt end was sad. Although we knew in the beginning we wouldn't be in Iran forever, letting go of our dreams wasn't easy. Sometimes, though, we have to relinquish the life we have planned through no fault of our own, and sometimes this means letting go of our dreams.

But, the universe is vast. There are other places to go, other people to meet, and other dreams to make. From the dreams that have passed us by, others will come to life, as we reflect and feed our spirit from what we've learned.

Sometimes, it's time to let go of the life we envisaged. Time to move forward and time to dream new dreams. Time to start fresh and new again. Time for the magic to begin again.

Leaving Isfahan

D AWN HADN'T YET BROKEN, WHEN we were hurried on to one of several big, blue Iranian buses parked outside the front door of the Khorosh Hotel. Our chaperons advised us to keep a low profile and avoid looking out the windows on our ride to the airport. They cautioned us to take all precautions, so we wouldn't be recognized as Americans by the Shah's military or Islamic extremists on the streets. Rumors had spread that many of the Shah's armed forces had begun aiding the ranks of the opposition, so we were told not to trust any Iranian, no matter how harmless they seemed.

As the bus neared the airport, we came upon a group of laborers working along the road in the ditches. The bus slowed to make its way around them. Curious, several workers wearing dusty turbans swiftly approached the bus. One jumped up and grabbed the window's edge. His feet dangled off the ground as he held on tight, straining to see through the foggy glass. The worker suddenly realized the bus was transporting Americans. His turban tumbled off his head, as his fingers slipped from the window edge, and he fell to the ground. Scrambling to get back on his feet, he shouted something to the other workers in Farsi, which we couldn't clearly understand. Without a moment's hesitation, the other men abandoned their picks and shovels, and raced toward the bus. My body slipped further down into the seat for fear of what would happen next. But our Iranian bus driver heard what the man had said and he clearly understood the workers' intentions. He abruptly floored the gas pedal, leaving the laborers standing behind us in a burst of dust. The workers chased the bus yelling, "Yankee, go home!" over and over again, while hurling rocks and dirt at us until the bus was completely out of sight.

Sometimes a situation in our life becomes so clear, we can no longer deny that we need to do something to take us away from the circumstance. Other people may give us subtle hints that we are no longer welcome in their lives. They may notice that we aren't listening, so they begin to speak louder. They begin to openly emphasize their intolerance toward us until, finally, we understand that it's time for us to leave the situation and take care of ourselves.

But we need to listen—really listen—to our own intuition. We need to learn to recognize for ourselves when a situation is wrong for us, before it's too late. Sometimes we even need to speed up the process and not ignore the inevitable.

Learn to recognize when something disquieting is happening around you. Don't deny the tugs and pulls on your spirit. Follow your intuition. You will know when a situation isn't right for you. You will instinctively know when it's time to go.

THE STEPS

FINALLY ARRIVING SAFE AND SOUND at the new, partially built airport near Toufanian High School, we were hurried off the bus to a waiting airplane on the deserted runway. To our surprise, a team of United States Special Forces lined each side of the steps. They stood tall and were dressed in full U.S. military greens with machine guns at their sides.

Extremely alert to everything happening all around them, the servicemen quickly guided us up the boarding steps of the plane. That's when it hit me. Reality finally sank in and I realized how dangerous the situation was in Iran. But I felt comforted, knowing the best of our country's servicemen were risking their lives with pride and honor to secure our safety for the journey back home.

Leaving the servicemen standing behind us, we stepped off Persian soil just as we'd stepped on it. Our last glimpse of Ed, Shawn, and the other American men was seeing them throw our luggage into the lower compartment of the plane.

We settled in our seats as the pilot strengthened the plane's power for an emergency takeoff. In an instant, the air pressure tightened and pulled at our faces as the nose of the plane shot straight up into the sky. We were gone.

Cheers of relief roared from other passengers on the plane but, for me, only a quiet sadness came. I knew I couldn't hold the political issues against the Iranian people. It was too late. I was returning home to America with Persia forever captured in my heart.

Sometimes it's once again time for change. The change may not be exactly what we expect, but others are always there to meet us and to help guide us to where we need to be. They make our journey more comfortable. They help us find our way back home.

At that moment, we might not understand the importance of those people's presence in our lives, and how, in some small or large way, their actions or words helped guide us to where we are today. Only later, when we look back on our past, do we understand and are truly thankful that those people were there, on our path, to help us along the way.

A Flight's Reflections

I LOOKED OUT THE TINY PORTHOLE as the plane leveled out into the sky, hoping to see my last winter sunrise over Isfahan, but all I could see was an empty desert in the fading night. So, I laid my head back and closed my eyes. And there, in the stillness of my mind, a picture of Isfahan, framed in purple mountains, silently unfolded. The halo of light over the Royal Mosque began to tug at my heart as I struggled to find a balance between the fear I felt and my love for the country that had graced my life.

As the picture became clearer, I began to understand the delicate balance in God's garden on the mountain back home. How each seed has a purpose beneath the soil and under the sun, and, if left undisturbed, in time, its season will come, naturally unveiling the color of its blossoms for all to see, freed from the earth to the sun.

So, accepting with faith the display of God's grace, I opened my eyes again, knowing, someday, life in Iran would be better. Perhaps then I would return to Isfahan and look over God's garden for a second time. Maybe then the little girls would, once again, run freely through the *koches,* the chadors falling from their faces, magically surrendering their blossoms to the warmth of the sunshine and a little spring rain. Perhaps then God would reveal for the whole world to see, through the little girls' hearts, the colors beneath the veil.

Lay your head back. Close your eyes. Quiet yourself. Rest. Now listen. Listen to the silence of your heart. See God moving and breathing in each experience and each story in your life.

Maybe we should all ponder the thought that what happened in Iran and continues to happen around the world—and in our own lives—is a simple lesson, the lesson of disturbing the seeds in God's garden.

We can't always understand what God has planned. But we can accept with faith that what's happening in our life is only a small part of a bigger plan. Even in the bleakness of winter and the darkness of night, we must have faith that God's grace is moving, working, and creating His garden. But, seeds can't be forced to blossom, they must grow naturally. If we're patient, maybe someday we'll see why it's all meant to be that way.

Maybe it's time to let God's garden be, knowing the seasons will turn and the seeds will find their way to the sunshine, revealing their blossoms where they were meant to be. Then, maybe, we'll never have to ask, "Which seed is the most significant on this Earth?" because we'll know each seed has its own special place and purpose in this world. They are all the reflection of God's grace.

Home Again

I STEPPED ON THE FRONT PORCH of my family's old, white house. I was so happy to be home but, as I look out over the valley, everything looked different. Even through the gray skies and pouring rain, life appeared more vivid, more alive, and much more colorful than before. Only the evergreen-laced mountains surrounding me seemed somewhat smaller. Everything was the same, yet somehow different, through my eyes. The feeling was something I couldn't yet explain.

From the corner of my eye, I glimpsed the old, weathered rose trellis at the side of the house, where rose vines lay dormant, draped over the familiar words painted on the white picket sign that hung on top the front of the lattice. I'd memorized these words by heart as a little girl—*One is nearer to God's heart in the garden than anywhere else on Earth*. These words meant much more to me that day than ever before.

A deep sense of gratefulness came over me when I opened the front door. Dad was placing kindling on hot coals in the fire-place as the aroma of mother's freshly baked bread filled the air throughout the house. There, in the warmth of my own home, I truly understand how fortunate Vance, Damon, and I were to be back on American soil, in the valley, with our families, safe, secure, and alive.

Although, I couldn't imagine who I would have been that day

without the story of the people and the country of Iran that had touched my life. It was as if my spirit would have been incomplete. The journey lifted the invisible veil from my eyes, giving me a new faith in the color of God's light. A faith, so true and pure and real that I trembled when the thought came to me—the only thing I know for certain about this journey through life is that after the winter rains have fallen, the sun will shine, and come spring the roses will bloom once again.

Tucked away in the corner of my heart is that idealistic girl I was in those days. I still ponder the magic and purpose of God's grace in my life, with each thought adding more color than the thought before. I believe this pondering fills my soul with God's light and what I choose to do with this light to enrich others' lives reflects the true spirit of His grace.

We are all, as individuals, a culture and a human race drawn to a different set of beliefs for a reason, a reason we may never know. So, we should all try to do our part to ensure a balance between growth, freedom, and preserving traditional ways. Then, maybe someday we will understand that even though we all come from a different place in the world, the same light is there to guide us all home—we just take different journeys to get there.

The End

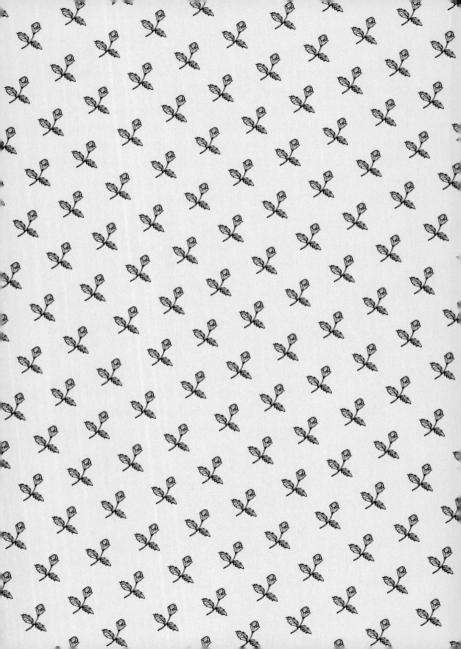

AFTERTHOUGHTS

O N JANUARY 16, 1979, TEN DAYS after our departure, and only a few days after Ed and Shawn's, the reign of the Pahlavi dynasty ended. Sickened with cancer and brokenhearted, Muhammad Reza Shah quietly flew into exile under the pretense of a lengthy vacation. Two weeks later, on February 1, 1979, Ayatollah Khomeini returned to his homeland to lead the country toward an Islamic-ruled nation—the Islamic Republic of Iran. As the Revolution drew to an end, the Iranian people, unable to bear witness to further bloodshed from their fellow countrymen, place flowers in the soldiers gun barrels. With the flower-capped guns slung over their shoulders, the soldiers walked the streets peacefully, signifying the Iranian's longing for peace and love among their people.

Since the country's transformation, two generations have come and gone, Khomeini and the Shah long ago passed away, and the Iranian Revolution is all but history. Yet, the world still stands witness to the long-lasting and powerful effects of religious fundamentalism forced on a nation and its people.

For now, though, one thing is certain—for whatever reason, God gave Khomeini's regime power over the Iranian people. Maybe, someday, the world will understand this mystery. I have faith though, that the Iranian people will, one day, free themselves from the fear that now imprisons their true Persian spirit. And, somewhere in the midst of it all, their dream of creating a balance between their ancient culture and the modern world will come to light. I hope the Iranians will discover for themselves their own unique place in this world, a place that isn't painted by the hands of the western world or religious fundamentalism, but that comes from the burning passion buried so deeply inside the soul of the Persian culture. Through it all, I hope God will reveal to the entire world how two distinct cultures can live side by side, in peace, in one world. Once again, reflecting that the freedom of our spirit is what allows our hearts to grow toward the light of love, and it's this love that will ultimately guide us to the true color of His glory and peace on Earth.

My Personal Reflection

THE ATTACKS ON THE PENTAGON and the World Trade Center in New York City transpired while I was writing this book. Throughout my writings, I have pondered many issues, but I have never struggled so hard to find perspective as I have from the tragic waste of human lives that occurred on September 11, 2001. Because of this, I feel a need to express my thoughts and concerns that surfaced from these events.

First, I know in my heart and through personal experience that what happened on September 11th was not the true spirit of the Islamic faith. Most Muslims I encountered in Iran and over the years have been kind, compassionate, peaceful, gracious, and loving people. We must not hold this tragic event against their religious faith.

Yet, through the total darkness, raging fires, billows of smoke, tears, and ashes, the question still lingers as to how such a vicious act could have happened. The simple, yet complicated, answer could be found in the abuse and use of mind control that has swept our world, unopposed, in the name of God throughout history, not only through Islam, but through Christianity and other spiritual faiths, too.

Maybe it's time for the human race to awaken to the true terror of any doctrine that preaches prejudice over justice and equality, justifies hatred over love and acceptance, and rationalizes isolation and control over freedom. We were badly shaken from the events of September 11th, but have we learned the lesson yet?

What other tragic event will we have to endure before we realize the power of religious fundamentalism and the consequences of its abuse? How many more lives will be lost, not only in body, but in spirit, too, before we have the passion and courage to stand up against it? We must open our eyes and see the powerful lesson learned from yesterday because, only then, can we begin to understand the answer and move forward, into the future, with a solution.

If I could shed any light on one lesson I learned from September 11th and my experience in Iran, it would be the need to teach children throughout the world how to reason with their own minds, to stop and think about whose voice and doctrine they're listening to. Fundamentalist views aren't inherent to human nature—those who care only about money, control, or power, not human souls, teach them. And, often, people who fall victim to these views are innocent and uneducated to their devastating effects on the body, the mind, and, the spirit.

We need to teach children to question those in authority who teach any doctrine that doesn't include tolerance, equality, and love for all human beings. We need to teach children to question the ideas of those who justify replacing our beliefs and freedom of thought with their beliefs and moral doctrine. Above all, we need to teach children to question those in authority who initiate fear, and not faith, in us, because ignorance is the seed of fear, fear is the foundation of hate, and hate is the root of violence.

If we can educate children to recognize the signs of an unhealthy doctrine, its cycle could be broken through those same children who stand up against it in generations to come. Then, maybe the whole world would reap the true power of knowledge from the seeds of faith it sprouts. Faith that grows into hope, and hope that plants the seeds of peace, joy, love, and acceptance.

I witnessed religious fundamentalism transform an entire nation and, every day, I'm confronted by its powerful effects on many people of different faiths within my own country. If we aren't careful, fundamentalist views could little by little take hold of our nation and transform the foundation of diversity from which America was born.

I hope you can grasp the magnitude of this crisis to the human race as a whole. I hope you can find enough interest in this subject to educate yourself, your children, and others of the tragic results that can occur when others are allowed to abuse their power with no boundaries and no empathy for others. I hope you can find within yourself the passion and courage to stand up against any abuses of power in the world around you, whether this is in your work place, your place of worship, or your home. Because, as individuals, we must each do our part to heal the world and to help prevent a tragic event reminiscent of September 11th, from ever happening again.

My sincere and heartfelt thoughts and prayers will always be with those who lost loved ones in the horrific events of September 11th—children, wives, husbands, mothers, fathers, grandparents, cousins, friends, neighbors, and acquaintances. They are all, the living and the dead, the victims of hatred created by the abuse of religious fundamentalism. This we must never forget.

Something
In your soul trusts
Me

Otherwise it would not let you near
These words.

God has spilled a Great One
Into each of us.

This warrior is always fearless
But also always
Kind.

The only business I am concerned
With these
Days,

Since I heard the Moon's
drunk
Singing,

Is
Stealing
Back our flute from
Krishna.

—*Hafiz, from* The Gift

OUR SILENT STORY

BURIED DEEP INSIDE EACH OF US lives a silent story yearning to be told. This is the beautiful story of our life, reflecting who we are and how our spirit came to be. This story is filled with lessons we've learned from people we've met along the way, and places we've been—not only places we've seen, but also places we've been deep inside our soul. This is a story only we can tell through our words, our eyes, and our heart of the love that has graced our lives.

Listen as the wide-eyed little boy tells his story, nervously searching for the perfect word to describe the magical moment when he witnessed a monarch butterfly unfolding from its cocoon. Or the frail old women who searches her memory, fighting to hold back tears that swell in her eyes as she reminisces about her journey through life and days gone by.

Inspirational stories unfold throughout our lifetime, each one touching our spirit in an extraordinary way. You may see them expressed on canvas in an artist's painting, feel them from the touch of a healer's hand, or hear them in the strumming of a musician's guitar or his lyrics to his song. Those inspiring stories—the ones that grab hold of our conscience and make us stop to ponder our purpose in life—are what add so much color to our spirit and depth to our soul. So, we must accept with faith that each place we go, each event we experience, and each person we meet has a purpose in our life, and, through this all, a story is created.

This is a story of God's graceful manner of forming our human soul, a soul with a purpose meant to be shared with others who enter our lives, so they can see the colors of our heart. Then, maybe through our words, our eyes, and our hearts, others may see the glory of God's light.

So, go inside yourself—to the depth of your soul—and know that you are at home. Go to the place inside yourself where it is quiet, where you find balance, and where you are at peace. Go to the place where you are safe to be who you were meant to be. The place that whispers to you—how you feel, what you see, how you believe—the place that whispers the truth unconditionally. Here you discover what your purpose is, what pleases you, what keeps your spirit alive. Here you can come to cherish, not to regret, the stories in your life. Find this place inside you. Be at home with it. Be it. Bring it to life. Then, gently, with all your courage, let it go. Release this place and let it be what it was meant to be. Set your spirit free. Surrender your purpose. Surrender your light to the world. And then, through your words, your eyes, and your heart let your story touch others' lives.

DEDICATIONS

TO MY TWO SONS, WARREN AND NICKOLAS—*thank you for your patience while I wrote this book, but most of all, thank you for the new colors you add to my life each day. I love you both with all my heart.*

TO MY MOTHER—*thank you for all your love and inspiration throughout my life. And thank you for having the wisdom and the courage to let go and allow me to experience a world so ancient and unknown, knowing how the journey would forever touch my life.*

TO ED AND NANCY—*my deepest gratitude for opening your home and your hearts to me, for accepting me as part of your family, and for sharing the experience of a lifetime. Without your generosity, my journey never would have been possible.*

TO SHAWN, DAMON, LYNN, KURT, AND HEATHER—*thank you for the special bond and the shared memories of love, tears, laughter, and music. You'll always be brothers and sisters to me.*

TO VANCE—*thank you for caring enough to share part of your life with me, and for your love, which will forever grace my life.*

TO DON—*thank you for your constant love, encouragement, and support throughout the years I struggled to make this book a reality. You'll always hold a very special part in my heart.*

TO MY SISTERS—*Candy, Nita, Gloria, Lori, Vicki, Julie, and Kim. And, to my brothers Pat, Jack, and Ivan—I love you all.*

TO MY FATHER AND MY BROTHER MIKE—*thank you for sharing your lives with us and for allowing us to understand the cycle of love, from beginning to end. My heart will be with you always.*

A SPECIAL THANK YOU TO MY IRANIAN FRIEND, MEHRADAD—*I appreciate your generosity in allowing me to use your poem in my book. But, most of all, thank you for being my friend.*

AND, TO THE PEOPLE I'VE MET ALONG THE WAY, ALL OF YOU WHO TOUCHED MY SOUL—*Thank you.*

With all my heart, I dedicate this book to you all.